Top Bananas!

BLOOMSBURY
LONDON · NEW DELHI · NEW YORK · SYDNEY

Top Bananas!

The best ever family recipes from Mumsnet

Claire McDonald and Lucy McDonald
crumbsfood.co.uk

Photography by Jill Mead

First published in Great Britain 2014

Text copyright © Mumsnet Limited 2014
Photography copyright © Jill Mead 2014

The moral right of the authors has been asserted

Bloomsbury Publishing Plc
50 Bedford Square, London WC1B 3DP

Bloomsbury Publishing, London,
New Delhi, New York and Sydney

ISBN 978 1 4088 5049 7

Mumsnet project editor: Catherine Hanly
Project editor: Lucy Bannell
Design: This-Side
Photography: Jill Mead
Food stylist: Bianca Nice
Props stylist: Polly Webb-Wilson

10 9 8 7 6 5 4 3 2 1

Printed and bound in China by C & C Offset
Printing Co. Ltd.

mumsnet.com
bloomsbury.com

Foreword
by Justine Roberts
Mumsnet founder and CEO

Our idea of what constitutes good mothering is intrinsically bound up with food. As soon as your offspring emerges, it is summarily weighed, measured and ranked by centile – and that centile chart, updated with weekly results and critical analysis from expert commentators, can quickly come to feel like an unforgiving yardstick of success. From the very first, parents are rudely awakened to their role as fierce competitors in the nutrition league.

Even if you get off to a flying start when your wee bairn graduates from milk to more substantial fare, there's no room for complacency. Many's the six-month-old who has greedily gobbled down bowlfuls of puréed courgette, or snaffled fistfuls of devilled olives from your plate, only for their conservative palate to kick in and catch you off-guard down the line. Before you know where you are, your repertoire of 'acceptable' meals has shrunk to nothing more than fish fingers, chips and rice-cake sandwiches.

Old Ben Franklin had a point when he said 'Fools make feasts and wise men eat them.'

I say, 'Better that they eat them than scream "No!" and chuck them across the room.'

And so it is that you find yourself pressing lumps of mild Cheddar into Hula Hoops in a desperate attempt to crowbar at least *some* protein into them... or hissing at your partner,

'Remember that it's turkey you're eating, not chicken,' because your child announced that they 'hate chicken' the day before.

How, you might ask yourself, did you get here? Children sense desperation. No matter whether you manage, by dint of extraordinary willpower and hours of practice in front of the mirror, to keep your voice low and your brow unfurrowed as you suggest that they aren't in fact allergic to all meats, fish, vegetables and fruits – they can smell it. So you take the path of least resistance, and reach for the fish fingers again.

Any of this ringing bells? Then this book is for you. It's brimful of recipes that have triumphed in the war against recalcitrant tastebuds and a deep scepticism of all things green; that have succeeded in halting the relentless march of spaghetti hoops and have allowed herbs, vegetables and, yes, even shellfish to creep (not literally) back on to the family dinner plate. Albeit often heavily disguised as tomato soup or pasta sauce.

What's more, these recipes are easy to make – really easy – and they don't cost the earth. You won't need to buy mountains of kitchen equipment to cook them, nor have to attend an advanced pastry-making course, nor source rare ingredients from far-flung corners of the world.

We are not worshipping at the altar of aduki beans and high tech water baths. Those are for the people with a little more time on their hands.

These are recipes that you can actually cook. They are healthier, cheaper and much more appetising than ready meals. You'll like them, and your family will, too. And if by chance they don't, you won't be rendered an insane screaming banshee because you've spent 24 hours sourcing truffle oil from remote uplands of Uzbekistan and then another two hours grating nutmeg.

How can we be so sure you'll like this cooking? Market research. Over the years, Mumsnet has grown into a repository of sure-fire recipes, each tried and tested by the fussiest of fussy eaters. And so the archives contain thousands to pick from... and we've picked the very best.

Of course we needed a professional eye to keep all the quantities correct and the instructions clear. Step forward the Crumbs sisters. Claire and Lucy, journalists both, are, in their own words, 'two sisters who like cooking and love eating'. After having children (four between them) they set up the Crumbs Food blog as 'a way of inspiring us to cook healthy, tasty, quick meals for our families'. So neatly did their philosophy – 'We give a two-breadstick salute to long ingredient lists and say hellooo to the culinary shortcut' – tally with our own, that a partnership seemed more or less preordained. Together with a wonderful group of volunteer Mumsnetters, the Crumbs have tested and retested every one of the recipes that appear in the book you're holding in your hands.

Cooking may become more complicated when children are around; your choice of ingredients might be more limited; your available hours curtailed. But it can also become more rewarding and satisfying and, if you don't mind the odd spillage, infinitely more fun. Eating a meal together – whether that's a three-course feast, pasta and pesto, or a plate of lopsided fairy cakes you spent the afternoon cobbling together – is cited on Mumsnet over and again as one of the great pleasures of family life. We hope that this book will help with that.

One final thought, courtesy of Nora Ephron, who sums everything up nicely, I think: 'I have made a lot of mistakes... and regretted most of them, but never the potatoes that went with them.'

Introduction

This isn't just a cookbook *for* you. It is a cookbook *by* you. We have spent the last four years, on our Crumbs Food blog and YouTube channel, talking to mums (and dads) about the challenges of family cooking. So when Mumsnet asked us to write a book about just that, using all the wonderful recipes and tips shared on their website, we jumped at the chance. Where better to look for such recipes than Mumsnet? Its food section is a library of thousands of recipes created by busy parents. It is family food gold.

We have four children between us and, although we love being mums, we still haven't quite mastered all the stuff that comes with it: the washing, the tidying, the continual running up and down stairs, not to mention the cooking. Before having children, we were keen home cooks who enjoyed rustling up three-course dinners and following complicated Sunday supplement recipes, but cooking soon lost its gloss amid the monotony of making three meals a day for a hungry and – often – unappreciative family. It became a chore, not a pleasure. Sound familiar?

We know what parents want from a cookbook because it is what we want, too. Tasty recipes that are easy to shop for and make, with short and uncomplicated ingredients lists.

So with all Mumsnet's recipes at our fingertips, we began our search for the best. The ones our family would want to eat over and over again.

This is where you came into the story. 'You' took the form of Mumsnetters who volunteered to test recipes and to tell us what you and your family really thought. Reactions ranged from the good: 'They went down a treat with children and adults alike,' to the OK: 'I don't like broccoli and was surprised how nice this was,' to the downright ugly: 'This tasted vaguely sickish.' You'll be glad to know that last one didn't make the final cut.

Then we cooked the recipes ourselves. Every single day, as we did so, our culinary repertoire grew. There was no time for fish fingers or oven chips. Our kids loved it: ice-cream-cone cakes? Yes *pleeeease*, they said. A sophisticated sea bass? Yes please, we said. Three-minute sponge? Simply a revelation. Cheese, tomato and thyme muffins and our children have never once met, we must confess. We see it as a simple timing glitch: always baked during the evening when the kids are already in bed, none of the muffins has yet made it through the night.

Every single one of these recipes has been exhaustively tested, first by Mumsnetters in their droves, and then by us. However, no recipe is foolproof; part of being a home cook is facing the fact that sometimes cakes will sink and gravies – inexplicably – won't thicken. It is not the end of the world. Even Delia has off days. Probably. The important thing is to learn from your mistakes and get back in that saddle.

These recipes are not ours, they are yours. We hope this collection will give you more confidence in the kitchen and that it will encourage you not just to follow a recipe, but to claim it as your own. So experiment, play around, add a little of what you fancy and subtract a little (or all) of what you don't.

Above all, enjoy.

Ingredients

The best food is always prepared with the best ingredients. This is not the same as the most expensive: supermarket own-label is often just as good as branded alternatives, only minus the marketing budget and posh packaging. What we mean is try to use food that is in season and freshly grown (if you do, it should both taste better and cost less than out-of-season, imported produce), though we know that this isn't always possible in the real world.

We use whatever milk we have in the fridge for these recipes, usually semi-skimmed or whole milk. As we are not making complicated patisserie, we find it doesn't really matter what colour the bottle top is.

All the eggs used in this book are large and free-range. We have used organic meat wherever possible. Yes, it costs more, but what price a happy pig? Just eat it less often. Nutritionists recommend eating less red meat anyway, so have a look at the Lovely Veggies chapter for scrumptious alternatives. We promise, you won't miss the meat one bit.

Unless otherwise stated, we use sea salt, freshly ground black pepper and olive oil.

Many of the recipes call for stock and we know that you'd have to eat a lot of chickens to have fresh stock at all times. So use whatever you have or prefer – cubes, pouches, bottles – we like those concentrated capsules the best.

For baking (and for icing!) use unsalted butter. And make sure your baking powder is fresh; once opened it goes off within a couple of months and that means your cakes won't rise. That is our excuse anyway.

With this book, if you have frozen peas, frozen prawns and frozen berries in your freezer; cheese, butter and milk in your fridge; and olive oil, pasta, honey, tinned tomatoes, tinned beans, tinned sweetcorn, eggs, lemons, rolled oats, lentils and ready-cooked noodles in your cupboard, you will never get caught out by the arrival of tea time again. That is a copper-bottomed promise.

Equipment

Listen up! You don't need to have any special paraphernalia to make the recipes in this book. This section is simply a guide to how you could make the cooking process easier, but it does involve spending money, so skip it if you want. However, in our opinion, not investing in kitchen kit can be a false economy. Anything that makes it easier to cook means less temptation to dial for a takeaway or to buy a microwave meal.

So first, get to know your kitchen equipment. We don't mean asking your blender its life story, but appliances vary – ovens in particular – so say hello and get to know yours. A good way to do this is by baking a sponge cake and then comparing its cooking time with the one stated in the recipe. You'll soon work out how your own oven compares and where its hotspots are. Even better, take the element of potluck out of baking and buy an oven thermometer: you might find you need to set your oven 10°C or so north or south of the temperature you want. No biggie.

Of course, we'd all love a large mixer where we could throw in all of the ingredients, saunter away and let it do all the work. But expensive deluxe models are hardly essential. And you need a lot of room to accommodate such a beast. What is vital for baking is an electric whisk, unless of course you are looking at cake-making as an economical alternative to gym membership. They are as cheap as chips – you can get them from most supermarkets for very little – and they take all the arm-ache out of creaming butter and sugar.

Blenders are worth their weight in gold. Great for smoothies and soups, they'll whizz up breakfast and lunch in seconds. Stand-alone blenders can look nice, but they mean more washing up than their hand-held counterparts, and they take up more counter space. A good solution to both your baking and blender needs is to buy a multi-use, hand-held blender that comes with blender, whisk and chopping blade attachments. Far cheaper than the alternatives. Plus it fits in the kitchen drawer.

Or buy a food processor. Really, do. They are the superheroes of the kitchen and can do the job of about ten other gadgets combined. They can slice, chop, grate and mix like demons. Some also come with a whisk attachment that is great for pancakes and cakes. Although it is a big investment, it is one you won't regret.

If your children are young, chances are your saucepans date back to when you were single or had just got together with your partner, so they are likely to be small and not suitable for a growing family. Supersize them. After all, you will be using them for the next twenty-odd years. Some things are worth spending money on.

Other useful bits and bobs include:

- Stainless-steel tongs. Perfect for everything from turning fish fingers, to plucking corn cobs out of boiling water, to tossing bowls of salad and pans of pasta.
- Silicone spatula for scraping bowls clean (when a finger just won't do).
- Nest of mixing bowls.
- Saucepan steamer for vegetables.
- Digital scales, so you can weigh both liquids and solids in the bowl you're going to mix them in, for less washing up.
- Freezer-bag pen and stickers. Freezing is next to godliness (and so is cleanliness, but it hasn't got the kudos), but not eating what you have frozen makes the whole endeavour a waste of time. So stop chiselling brown mush out of Tupperware boxes, hoping it is gravy and not chocolate sauce, and label and date each box. No one ever wants to eat something if they aren't sure what it is. Chicken stew is lovely, but not when you were expecting apple crumble.

Getting children to eat

We start off with such good intentions. Puréeing organic vegetables and sourcing salt-free stock cubes. The weaning process can feel like the start of a big adventure off into the foothills of flavour and texture. Yeah, right (hollow laugh). Because it's not long before children realise the power of 'No!' and start to assert their independence through food. And this is where one of life's biggest pleasures can turn into a true emotional battleground; an opportunity for tiny tots to exercise their dictatorial tendencies. *But it is a normal phase* and it's really important (though hard!) not to be upset by it. It will pass. We promise. In the meantime, here are some ways to reduce the collateral damage.

- Don't spend hours cooking just for them. Whizz something quick up, or give them something you are making anyway. That way it doesn't matter when they say 'No!' You haven't spent hours slaving away, so there isn't too much emotional fallout. Be lazy. It's allowed.

- Suppress your own dictatorial tendencies. Unless you're a nutritionist, the portion size you've given to them is probably arbitrary, so don't force them to eat up everything on their plate for the sake of it. Tea time will just become a battle of wills.

- Less is more when it comes to children's portion sizes. Piles of food can overwhelm. Give just a little, then allow them to help themselves to more if they want. This also gives them a bit of control, so they don't feel the need to exert it elsewhere.

- If kids won't eat a certain food, simply clear it away without comment. It's no biggie. Offer them fruit instead.

- It's important that children try new foods, but that doesn't have to mean a whole plate of runner beans. A small mouthful is fine. If they've tried it and don't want any more, they can leave the rest.

- When you have fussy eaters, keep all those biscuits, crisps and other treats off the menu. If they know you'll always give them something tasty between meals, it makes them more likely to refuse what is on their plate at lunch time.

- Use hunger! It's an extremely powerful tool. No snacks between meals = a child who is actually quite hungry at meal times. You'll be surprised at your success rate when trying a new – or previously refused – food if they are truly ravenous.

- Try not to make a big deal of puddings: sometimes you get them and sometimes you don't. They are not a reward for eating the main meal. In fact, avoid using food (including sweets) as a reward for anything. It just complicates the issue.

- Children often pick up eating habits from their family. That means you. So if you are constantly dieting or are a fussy eater, they are more likely to be picky, too.

Tips for feeding young children

- Babies and young children have small stomachs and high energy requirements. They should not be on high-fibre or low-fat diets, which can make it difficult for them to eat as many calories as they need.

- Cow's milk can be introduced to a baby's diet to make things such as sauces or custard from the age of six months, but, until your baby is twelve months old, they still need to be given breast or formula milk to drink, as cow's milk doesn't contain enough iron or other nutrients.

- Eggs can be given to babies when they are more than six months old, but make sure they are cooked until both white and yolk are solid.

- Don't give honey to your baby until they are one year old. Honey sometimes contains a type of bacteria that can produce toxins in babies' intestines.

- The NHS advises not giving any whole nuts, including peanuts, to children under the age of five because they could cause choking.

The health bit

One of a parent's most important jobs is to give their children a healthy balanced diet. Making sure yours eat a wide variety of foods, from all the different food groups, will ensure they get all the vital nutrients they need to grow up into veritable superheroes and save the world. Here are some basic nutritionists' guidelines to give you a steer.

Starchy carbohydrates

Bread, breakfast cereal, potatoes, pasta, rice, noodles, couscous.

Carbs contain protein, fibre, vitamins and minerals, but their main job is to provide energy. Carbohydrates should make up about one-third of the food on your child's plate and they'll need about four portions a day. They may moan, but try to get older children to eat wholemeal or granary breads, as they contain more of the fibre which is needed for healthy digestion. If they turn up their noses, fool them with white bread that is fortified with iron, or that half-and-half bread that is neither brown nor white.

Fruits and vegetables

Apples, bananas, pears, orange juice, tinned peaches, peas, lettuce, carrots, sweetcorn.

These are rich in vitamins, minerals, fibre and phytochemicals, all of which help ward off scurvy and should keep your children fighting fit. Phytochemicals – as the name suggests – are chemicals found in plants, such as lycopene and betacarotene, whch the plants use to protect themselves. A growing body of research suggests they can do us good, too, perhaps reducing the risk of cataracts, heart disease and certain types of cancer later in life.

Children who are more than five years old should eat at least five portions of a wide variety of fruit and vegetables every day, though the amount a child needs varies with age, body size and physical activity. As a rough guide, one portion is about the amount they can fit into the palm of their hand. Frozen, tinned and dried fruit or vegetables all count too, though fruit juice as only one portion, no matter how big the glass!

Many children find a mountain of vegetables off-putting, so you can start small. Think of a rainbow, and try to provide fruit or vegetables from the different colours each day. OK, maybe not blue, but you get the drift. Make a chart of all the types your children like at the end of the month. The next month get them to beat that number to win a treat. Some broccoli, maybe.

Meat and meat alternatives

Red meat, fish, eggs, beans and pulses, nuts and seeds.
All these foods provide the power-punch that is protein. This is essential for growth, repairing cells and the production of enzymes, antibodies and hormones. Protein also provides vitamins and minerals such as iron.

Growing children need two to four portions of meat or meat alternatives each day. If they eat fish – hurrah! – aim to serve it twice a week (frozen, tinned, fish fingers and fishcakes all count) and try to include oily fish – such as salmon, sardines and fresh tuna (tinned tuna doesn't count) – once a week, which will make them brainier.

Dairy products

Cheese, milk, yogurt, fromage frais.
As was hammered into us all at school, dairy contains calcium, which helps make bones and teeth strong. Gnash. Having enough calcium when children are young and growing fast will help to reduce the risk of osteoporosis later in life. Dairy products also contain protein, phosphorus, vitamin A, vitamin B2 and vitamin D.

Most children love dairy and getting them to eat three to four portions a day should not be too difficult, especially when you tell them

that yogurts, milkshakes and custard all count! One portion of dairy is equivalent to 200ml milk (about a tumbler), a matchbox-sized piece of cheese, or a 150ml pot of yogurt.

Children who are less than two years old should have whole milk. If your child has a good appetite, the NHS recommend switching to semi-skimmed milk at two and skimmed at five, since dairy products can be high in saturated fat.

Watch the salt

Children are more sensitive to the harmful effects of salt than adults, so ideally salt should never be added to food for babies and toddlers. Remember to check the nutrition information on any ready meals, snacks and cereals you give to children, because often the salt levels are much higher than you would think. This table shows an advised daily amount for your child's age.

Age (years)	Amount of salt per day (g)	Sodium (g)
1–3	2	0.8
4–6	3	1.2
7–10	5	2
11 and over	6	2.4

Foods containing fats and sugar

Margarine, butter, oils, biscuits, cakes, pastries, mayonnaise, bottled sauces, cream, ice cream, crisps, sweets, chocolates, jam and honey, sugary drinks.
Now, the tricky part. Our bodies are hard-wired to like fat and sugar, but these foods shouldn't be eaten too often, and only then in small amounts.

Very low-fat diets are not advisable for young children, because they need fat for energy. Try to choose healthy fats such as avocado, olive oil and oily fish instead of, ummm... chocolate and ice cream. Or even chocolate ice cream. To reduce the risk of tooth decay, sugary foods and drinks should be eaten only at meal times.

The right and wrong kinds of fat

Of all the nutrients in our diet, fat must be the most debated *and* most misunderstood. Although, in terms of healthy eating, fat is often cast as villain, it also plays a beneficial role. In the body, fat cushions and protects vital organs, provides energy and helps to insulate us. In terms of diet, fat is necessary for the absorption of some vitamins (A, D, E and K) and to provide essential fatty acids. These fatty acids are important for good health but, as the body cannot make them, they need to come from your diet.

The problem is that many of us are eating too much of the wrong fat and not enough of the right fat. Fats come in different varieties, which nutritionists divide into two main groups called saturated and unsaturated fats (this group can be further divided into monounsaturated and polyunsaturated).

Saturated fats such as butter, ghee or lard tend to be solid at room temperature, while the unsaturated fats such as olive oil and rapeseed oil tend to remain liquid at room temperature. But the differences don't end there; the type of fat you eat can also affect your health. A diet high in saturated fats is known to increase the risk of heart disease and stroke, which is why nutritionists urge us all to make simple changes to our diet which will help to reduce our intake.

Low-fat diets may not be suitable for very young children but, even for them, too much saturated fat is not good; it can cause problems such as heart disease further down the line.

Food allergies

Dairy, wheat, shellfish and nut allergies are more common in children than adults, and seem to be on the rise, along with other less common dietary allergies. They tend to run in families and can be temporary or life-long. If you suspect your child has an allergy, it's important to seek professional help rather then diagnosing them yourself. If you're not careful, cutting out a major food group such as wheat or dairy can lead to nutritional deficiencies. So ask your doctor for an appointment with a registered dietitian.

Vegetarian children

A vegetarian diet can easily provide everything a growing child needs. But it is important to understand that meat offers essential nutrients, which need to be sourced from other foods if you or your child avoid meat. Look at the Resources section (see page 314) for where to find information on creating a healthy vegetarian diet.

10 tips to help kids eat healthily

1. Discourage eating meals or snacks while watching TV. Try to eat only in designated areas of your home, such as in the dining room or kitchen. Eating in front of the TV will distract children so that they don't notice their natural feelings of fullness, which can lead to overeating.

2. Make sure your child has regular meal times and snacks, rather than grazing continually. Endless snacks don't deliver a good balance of nutrients, and snack foods are often high in fat, sugar or salt.

3. A healthy breakfast is particularly vital for children, so make sure they don't skip the first meal of the day. Studies show that children who eat breakfast tend to have a higher intake of key vitamins and minerals. Many breakfast cereals are fortified and the milk they are eaten with provides calcium, which is crucial for their growing bones. Children who don't eat breakfast find it a bit more difficult to concentrate in the morning, which is why many schools run breakfast clubs.

4. Make an effort to eat together as a family at least twice a week. Turn off the television and keep conversations around the table happy... save the lectures for another time.

5. Don't forget that kids learn by example, so set a good one and eat a well-balanced diet yourself.

6. Make healthy eating fun. Try keeping a star chart, for example, awarding one star for each new type of vegetable eaten. Offer a treat when your child reaches ten stars.

7. A good time to introduce new or healthy foods is when your child is hungry. Most kids are ravenous when they get home from school in the afternoon, so this is a good time for you to pounce!

8. When your child says they're hungry, offer fruit. Only when they've eaten that can they have something else. Don't give in to pestering: be firm, anticipate moments when you are likely to be asked for the 'wrong' foods and have healthy alternatives ready, especially on trips to the shops.

9. Don't let children fill up on fizzy drinks or squash in between meals. Drinks can be quite filling – as well as surprisingly high in sugar and very fattening – and will reduce a child's appetite at meal times.

10. Teach kids that cooking can be creative and fun. Children learn best by doing, not watching, so get them involved! Getting them to help prepare meals can teach important skills such as shopping and cooking, weights, measures and numbers, and provides a good opportunity for them to learn about healthy eating. Turn to our Cooking with Children chapter (see page 212) for some inspiration.

Breakfast

Top ten!

- **Banana pancakes**
- **Perfect Monday morning porridge**
- **Not-just-for-Rudolph cranberry granola**
- **Bionic smoothie**
- **Fluffy eggs**
- **Eggy doorstops**
- **Kedgeree**
- **Devils-on-horseback bread**
- **Breakfast quesadilla**
- **Potato latkes**

You've learned a lot since having your first child. How to put a nappy on (them); how to deal with sleep deprivation (you); then there's weaning and potty training. By the time you've got over those hurdles, you will almost certainly have read several thousand child-rearing manuals and websites which, among many other gems, will have informed you that 'breakfast is the most important meal of the day'. Apparently an espresso and a fag are a real no-no, and you should give your children something more wholesome. But what?

According to nutritionists, the ideal breakfast should be a balance of slow-release carbohydrates, protein, vitamins and minerals (particularly calcium) and at least one piece of fruit. But what does that mean in real terms?

Porridge. Yup, it's the middle class's Holy Grail. Porridge for breakfast, muesli if you're feeling daring. It's that slow-release energy which keeps our stomachs feeling full for longer. Throw in a handful of chopped fruit and you've already got one of your five-a-day. A sprinkling of nuts adds the protein. Cook it with milk and you've increased the amount of calcium your children receive, helping to maintain healthy bones and teeth. Apparently we get through 47 million gallons of the stuff each year... perhaps that's because it lowers cholesterol, helps prevent heart disease and makes you happy (well, boosts serotonin).

But we couldn't fill a chapter on breakfast with porridge recipes: porridge with banana; porridge with cinnamon; porridge with pears and ginger... it gets repetitive. You'd probably feel you weren't getting your money's worth.

So, instead, these are breakfasts for high days and holidays, weekends, birthdays, lazy bank holidays and the odd special occasion. With some good ideas (and one porridge recipe for Monday mornings) thrown in.

Whatever day it is, experts agree that breakfast should provide 20–25 per cent of your total energy and nutrition needs; that's 400–500 calories for an adult. That's why, when it comes to breakfast, you should think big. A tiny portion of bought cereal doesn't really cut it, and although you may not feel like knocking up Potato latkes on a wet Wednesday morning before the school run (fair enough), something simple such as a Bionic smoothie or Not-just-for-Rudolph cranberry granola are an easy way to raise your game.

But at the weekend it's another matter. Getting the kids out of the front door requires discipline, dedication and – more often than not – threats. How often do you manage to leave the house and realise it's 11.30am and you're all going to need lunch soon? Or is that just us? Anyway, a good way to avoid a pricey visit to a café almost immediately after leaving the house is a hearty breakfast or brunch.

So save the latkes and the Breakfast quesadillas for then. Kedgeree and Fluffy eggs are both jam-packed with protein, so they're perfect for a long day out and will keep you full for ages. Devils-on-horseback bread can be made well in advance, then whipped out of the freezer as a deliciously savoury morning treat. These substantial breakfast and brunch recipes mean you need never stop off for an emergency fast food lunch again. Well, not unless you really want to...

Banana pancakes

Makes 8

For the pancakes
225g plain flour
1 tsp baking powder
300ml milk
2 eggs, lightly beaten
Pinch of caster sugar
Salt
2 ripe bananas, sliced
1 tbsp (15g) unsalted butter

To serve
Honey
Maple syrup
Chocolate spread

 Vegetarian

If all the world's dictators ate pancakes for breakfast, there would be no more wars, economic meltdowns or parking tickets. Everyone would happily go about their business, kicking their heels in the air.

In case you didn't get that, we like pancakes here at Mumsnet Towers. We could eat them for breakfast, lunch and dinner. These come with in-built sliced banana and are especially good. The batter doesn't keep well (the bananas turn limp) so it is best used straight away. Believe us, that won't be a problem.

1. In a large bowl, use a balloon whisk to whisk the flour, baking powder, milk, eggs, sugar and a pinch of salt together until the mixture is smooth. When there is not a lump in sight, gently fold the bananas into the batter.

2. Melt a teaspoon of the butter in a large frying pan and, when sizzling (don't let the butter brown or burn), spoon small ladlefuls of batter into the pan in pancake-shaped splodges, making sure each pancake has at least a couple of slices of banana in it. They're meant to be the size of Scotch pancakes, not crêpes, so you should be able to get three in there without them touching.

3. Once small bubbles have risen to the surface of a cooking pancake, flip it over using a fish slice, palette knife or spatula. When both sides are golden brown, the pancakes are ready to eat. Remove from the pan and either serve immediately, or stack on a plate and keep warm while you cook the rest. (The best way is to put a single layer on a plate in an oven preheated to 150°C/fan 130°C/gas mark 2.) You may have to increase or reduce the heat under the pan, especially for subsequent batches, to get an even colour on the pancakes without scorching.

4. Drizzle the gilded banana-y loveliness with honey (though don't give honey to children less than one year old, see page 14), or maple syrup, or even serve chocolate spread on the side.

Perfect Monday morning porridge

Serves 1 adult

For the porridge

1 teacup porridge oats
1 teacup water,
  plus more if needed
1 teacup milk,
  plus more to serve
Salt

Choose your flavourings and toppings

Muscovado sugar
Ground ginger
Ground cinnamon
Pear, cored and chopped
Apple, cored and chopped
½ banana, sliced
Blueberries
Honey
Flaked almonds
Handful of sunflower
  seeds, toasted in a dry pan
Plain yogurt

❦ Vegetarian

There are those who believe that only stirring clockwise will give you perfect porridge (*and* get rid of the devil). Here at Mumsnet we don't give a spurtle for such old wives' tales. We believe that putting hot porridge on the breakfast table before school is as close as we'll get to sainthood. And the only way to do that is with an easy recipe made with the minimum of fuss. That's why these measurements are in cups (and we're talking nice teacups rather than hefty builder's mugs), because no one wants to weigh things out at 7.30am. Just scale the amounts up according to how many you are cooking for.

1. Put a small saucepan on the hob and pour in the oats. Add the water and milk and turn on the heat.

2. Stir the porridge to stop it sticking to the pan. The higher the heat, the more you need to stir to stop it sticking; ideally keep it on a gentle heat so it doesn't become glue-like.

3. After about five minutes, add a pinch of salt. Cook for a bit longer if you think the oats need it, adding more water if it looks a bit dry.

4. Once cooked, stir in sugar and spices if you're using them, to taste.

5. Add a splash of milk to loosen up the porridge, spoon into bowls and then sprinkle fruit, honey, nuts, seeds or yogurt – or a combination – over the top. (Remember not to give honey to children less than one year old, nor whole nuts to children less than five years old, see page 14.) Bada-bing! Healthy living in a bowl, and your first small step to that halo.

Not-just-for-Rudolph cranberry granola

Makes about 15 decent adult-sized breakfasts, depending on greed

500g porridge oats
100g flaked almonds
100g desiccated coconut,
   or dried coconut flakes
3 tbsp light brown sugar
3 tbsp unsalted butter,
   melted, or vegetable oil
1 tsp ground cinnamon
1 tsp vanilla extract
Salt
130g maple syrup
50g dried sweetened
   cranberries (or another
   dried fruit if you'd prefer)
50g raisins

♥ Vegetarian

♥ **The health bit**
The best thing about making your own granola or muesli is that you have complete control over what goes in it… oh, the power! So play around with the sugar-to-fruit ratio until you're happy that the granola tastes sweet because of all that lovely fruit, rather than because of the syrup.

If Father Christmas gets mince pies and sherry, why shouldn't Rudolph get a handful of this? (But only if he's good, because there is a certain amount of faff involved; at least, more faff than opening a pack of muesli.) The effort is paid back by the most delicious breakfast this side of Christmas.

Have it with milk for breakfast, with yogurt and fruit compote for pudding, or by the handful just because you're passing the jar. Apparently, leftover granola will keep in an airtight container for about a month… you'll be lucky if it lasts a week.

1. Preheat the oven to 150°C/fan 130°C/gas mark 2.

2. Put the oats, almonds, coconut, sugar, melted butter or oil, cinnamon and vanilla into a large bowl and add a pinch of salt. Using a large spoon (or your hands, if you want to get all Nigella), work in the maple syrup until you can't see it any more.

3. Line two large baking trays with greaseproof paper and divide the granola mix between them. Place the trays in the hot oven and bake for 25 minutes, giving both trays a good stir halfway through, spooning the golden oats from the outside edge into the centre, and swapping the positions of the baking trays so they cook evenly. The idea is that the granola toasts to an even golden brown, so depending on your oven it may take longer than 25 minutes, just keep an eye on it. You do not want any black bits, so watch it like a hawk.

4. Remove the trays from the oven and let cool before stirring in the cranberries and raisins. When it's completely cold, store the granola in an airtight container.

Bionic smoothie

Serves 1 adult

1 banana, nice and ripe,
  roughly sliced
1 tbsp – or more if you
  like – crunchy or smooth
  peanut butter
250ml milk

For a very berry smoothie

Handful of berries, such as
  raspberries, blueberries
  or strawberries (fresh or
  frozen work well)
1 banana, nice and ripe,
  roughly sliced
Milk, juice or yogurt
Ice (optional)

❤ Vegetarian

♥ **The health bit**

At those times when a
chocolate bar is winking at
you, these also make super
snacks. Throwing in a couple
of tablespoons of oats boosts
their nutritional impact. You
can substitute goat's milk,
oat or rice milk... if you or
your children are lactose-
intolerant, you know the drill.

Super-quick, super-easy, super-delicious. This is the powerhouse
of the smoothie world and a healthy way to start the morning. The
peanut butter (trust us!) packs a protein punch that will keep you
going until lunch and the banana, well, it needs no introduction.
A smoothie wouldn't be a smoothie without one.

  Incidentally, peanut butter and sliced banana on toast is another
of our breakfast favourites, although eating it with the smoothie
could be too much of a good thing.

1. Place the banana, peanut butter and milk in a blender and purée until
the mixture is smooth.

2. Pour into a tall glass.

3. Straw optional.

To make a very berry smoothie

Take the berries and pop them in a blender with the banana and enough
milk, juice or yogurt to create a smoothie-like consistency. Whizz, with
some ice, if you used fresh berries. If you used frozen berries, you won't
even need any ice. Bob's your uncle. Breakfast. And you can freeze this
smoothie in lolly moulds to make implausibly healthy ice lollies.

Fluffy eggs

Serves 1–2 adults

2 slices of bread, crusty
   or pre-sliced, whatever
   you have in the house
60g Cheddar cheese, or
   other hard cheese, grated
2 eggs, separated

♥ Vegetarian

♥ The health bit

Aside from tasting great,
eggs are an excellent source
of protein and are brilliant
at keeping you feeling full
for longer. Plus, they're one
of the few foods stuffed
with vitamin D, which is
important for the absorption
of calcium and for healthy
bones. And while sun on our
skin helps our bodies make
vitamin D, that only works
in the summer. So between
October and March (or all
year round if the British
summer fails to materialise),
we need to look elsewhere
for our vitamin D. Eggs are
the answer.

**Without wanting to blow our own trumpet, these are amazing.
Eggs on toast as made by the gods, they resemble savoury
cloud-like meringues… but nicer.**

1. Preheat the oven to 200°C/fan 180°C/gas mark 6.

2. Lightly toast the bread, then lay the slices on a baking tray and sprinkle
the grated cheese on top.

3. Put one egg yolk on each slice of bread.

4. Whisk the egg whites with an electric mixer until they form soft peaks.
Spoon the whites over each slice of bread, smoothing so they cover the
whole surface more or less evenly.

5. Bake in the hot oven for 10–15 minutes, until they go a bit golden and
look set. For young children, babies and pregnant women, cook until you
are sure the egg yolk is cooked through (cut a piece open to check). Serve
with ketchup. Lots and lots of ketchup.

Eggy doorstops

Serves 4 adults

3 eggs
Splash of milk
Salt and pepper
4 slices of day-old bread,
  the thicker the better
8 rashers of streaky bacon
A little maple syrup, plus
  more to serve
Unsalted butter, to fry
Cherry tomatoes
  (optional)

♥ **The health bit**

It is best to use wholemeal or granary bread, but don't sweat it if your little ones will only eat the white stuff. It may not have as much fibre, but these days it is usually fortified with iron and calcium in any case.

There is so much to love about eggy bread: it is perfect for using up slightly past-it loaves; it is a good way of getting children to eat a substantial breakfast... oh, and it is deliciously easy.

Adding some crisp rashers of bacon makes this a wonderful weekend breakfast. Maple syrup compulsory.

If you're feeling flash, roast some cherry tomatoes in olive oil, salt and pepper for about 20 minutes in an oven preheated to 180°C/fan 160°C/gas mark 4 and serve them alongside.

1. In a large shallow bowl (big enough to lay the bread slices in) beat the eggs with the milk and some salt and pepper. Soak the bread in the egg mixture until wet but not too soggy; you don't want it to fall apart.

2. Meanwhile, brush the bacon rashers with a little maple syrup. Grill the rashers until really crisp, turning over halfway.

3. Melt a knob of butter in a large frying pan. When it's sizzling, carefully fry the bread a slice at a time, turning once with a fish slice when the underside is golden. Keep the cooked eggy doorstops warm in a single layer on a plate in an oven preheated to 150°C/fan 130°C/gas mark 2 while you cook the rest. You may have to increase or reduce the heat under the frying pan, especially for the subsequent batches, so the slices end up golden rather than singed...

4. When all are cooked, serve with the crisp sweet bacon on the top and a large glug of maple syrup. Add the tomatoes, if you want, or roast them first (see recipe introduction) and serve alongside.

Kedgeree

Serves 4 adults

60g unsalted butter
Large pinch of turmeric
1 clove
Seeds from 1 green
  cardamom pod
225g long-grain rice
600ml hot fish or
  chicken stock
2 eggs
300ml milk
1 onion, sliced
1 bay leaf
2 black peppercorns
400g smoked haddock
  (or a sustainable white fish
  such as coley, if your kids
  don't like smoked fish)
Handful of parsley leaves,
  roughly chopped
Lemon wedges, to serve
Salt and pepper

♥ **The health bit**

This dish can be part of a
cunning plan to sneak in veg.
Try peas first and, once your
kids get used to seeing those
in there, you can break out
the more adventurous stuff:
stir in some baby leaf spinach
or a spot of watercress.

This may have been eaten for breakfast in the days of the Raj, when there were servants to make it, but in this day and age it's probably ambitious to expect anyone to make (or eat) kedgeree before the school run. It's the perfect weekend brunch though, especially if you are out for the day. All that protein means you'll keep going until mid-afternoon... and you won't need to feel guilty when everything slides and the kids have candyfloss and crisps for tea.

1. Preheat the oven to 200°C/fan 180°C/gas mark 6.

2. Put a large ovenproof pot (one that has a lid) over a medium heat. As it heats up, add the butter. Once that has melted, add the turmeric, clove and cardamom seeds. Stir in the rice, cook for one minute, then add the hot stock and bring to the boil. Put the lid on and put the pot in the oven for 15–20 minutes.

3. Bring a small pan of water to the boil, lower in the eggs, return to the boil and cook for seven minutes. Remove them from the pan and cover with cold water, to stop them cooking. When they're cool enough to handle, peel them. Set aside.

4. Meanwhile, pour 600ml of water into a deep sauté or frying pan. Add the milk, onion, bay leaf and peppercorns. Bring to the boil, then slide in the fish, reduce the heat to a simmer and poach for 10 minutes, or until the flesh is opaque and flakes easily from the skin. Remove the fish from the liquid with a fish slice, discard the skin and flake into large chunks, checking for bones and throwing them away as you do so.

5. Take the rice out of the oven; it should have absorbed all the stock and be perfectly cooked. Gently stir in the fish, being careful not to break it up.

6. Serve scattered with parsley, allowing everyone half a boiled egg and a wedge of lemon. Season to taste (a generous grind of pepper is good).

7. Feel smug that your child has filled up with healthy food and it isn't even lunchtime.

Devils-on-horseback bread

Unsalted butter, for
  greasing the tin
200g bacon lardons, or
  streaky bacon, chopped
3 eggs, lightly beaten
150g self-raising flour
100ml flavourless oil,
  such as vegetable oil
120ml milk
150g pitted prunes,
  roughly chopped
100g hard cheese, grated
  (whatever you prefer,
  or have in the fridge)

👉 You will need
1-litre loaf tin.

❋ Freezable

Some people use air freshener. Others pop on some coffee to fill their houses with a beautiful aroma. We use bacon. Who doesn't love the smell of cooking bacon? Even veggies have a sneaky sniff when they think no-one's looking. This bread will not only fill your home with an exquisite smell, it combines bacon with prunes. Genius.

1. Preheat the oven to 180°C/fan 160°C/gas mark 4. Lightly butter a one-litre loaf tin.

2. In a dry frying pan, fry the lardons or bacon until nicely browned.

3. Meanwhile, mix the eggs and flour in a bowl. Pour in the oil and mix. It will look like a big oily, gloopy mess... but stay with us, it will be fine. Bit by bit, add the milk and keep stirring until it's well mixed together. The consistency should now look a bit more reassuring! Stir in the cooked bacon, the prunes and cheese.

4. When everything is well mixed, pour into the prepared loaf tin and pop into the hot oven for 45 minutes.

5. Take out of the oven when a skewer comes out clean, let it cool a little, then turn out of the tin and pop on a wire rack to cool. This is particularly great when used as soldiers with soft-boiled eggs, but is also lovely on the side with any hot breakfast, or just on its own.

Breakfast quesadilla

Serves 2 adults

1 sausage
2 eggs
Salt and pepper
1 tsp unsalted butter
2 flour tortillas
250g cheese (strong
  Cheddar is good), grated
4 spring onions, sliced
1 tomato, finely chopped
Guacamole or sour cream,
  to serve

♥ **The health bit**
If you want to offset the
sausages and cheese a bit,
try using low-fat versions,
and swap in natural yogurt
for the sour cream.

If you feel stuck in a full-English rut with your weekend breakfasts, then this Mexican-style quesadilla could be a welcome refresher. It is just a little bit different and every last morsel of it is delicious. The normal breakfast ingredients of eggs, sausage and bread are all there, just in a different format. For adults, it goes very well with a Bloody Mary alongside. Not that we are recommending that on a school day... not on paper, anyway.

1. Grill the sausage until it is browned all over, then slice it.

2. Make scrambled eggs: in a small bowl, lightly beat the eggs with some salt and pepper, and melt the butter in a small saucepan over a medium heat. Add the eggs and stir with a wooden spoon – being sure to go right into the corners of the pan – until *just* set, with no runny egg. Make sure you don't overcook them, as they will continue to cook in the next stage.

3. Place a large, dry frying pan over a medium heat and add a tortilla. Sprinkle over the cheese, add the scrambled eggs and finally the sausage. Once the cheese has started to melt, add the spring onions and tomato.

4. Top with the other tortilla and put a large plate over the frying pan. Wearing oven gloves and holding on to both plate and pan firmly, invert the whole lot (be *very* careful of your hands and arms, in case of splashing hot oil and/or cheese). The tortilla will land on the plate. Put the pan back over the heat and slide back the tortilla, uncooked-side down.

5. Once cooked, the quesadilla will look lightly browned and the cheese will have melted. Remove it from the pan and cut into wedges. Season to taste and eat with guacamole or sour cream on the side.

Potato latkes

Makes 12–15, enough for
4 hungry adults

For the latkes
100g plain flour
2 eggs, lightly beaten
1 small onion, grated
4 baking-type potatoes
   (about 800g in total)
Salt and pepper
½ tsp freshly
   grated nutmeg
Vegetable oil, to fry

For the eggs (optional)
1 egg per person
Malt or white wine vinegar

Other nice things, to serve
Sour cream
Chopped chives
Smoked salmon
Roast cherry tomatoes
   (see page 34)

❦ Vegetarian

✳ Freezable
Cool the latkes completely
after cooking. Open-freeze
in a single layer, then transfer
to a freezer bag for storage.
Reheat them in a single layer in
an oven preheated to 180°C/
fan 160°C/gas mark 4 for
15 minutes, until hot through.

These are delicious; perfect Sunday brunch fodder. Invite your favourite veggie friends round for a fry-up and they will be so relieved not to be served vegetarian sausages, they'll be putty in your hands for life. Even fussy children like these, so consider doubling the quantities and freezing any that aren't scarfed down immediately. (Apparently that can happen. Just not to us.)

If you're preparing these for friends, make them in advance, then keep them warm in the oven for up to 30 minutes. This way you'll actually be able to talk to your guests rather than simply communing with a hot frying pan.

1. Tip the flour, eggs and onion into a large bowl and mix thoroughly. Peel the potatoes, grate them in and season it all with salt, pepper and nutmeg. Bear in mind that potatoes on their own are pretty flavourless, so you probably need quite a lot of seasoning. Mix well.

2. Put a large saucepan of water on for the poached eggs, if using. (Don't serve poached eggs to babies, very young children or pregnant women unless they are cooked hard.)

3. While the water is reaching the boil, preheat the oven to 150°C/fan 130°C/gas mark 2. Cover the base of a large frying pan with vegetable oil, place over a medium heat and, when the pan reaches a moderate heat, drop 1 large tbsp of potato mixture into the pan. Flatten it with the back of a spoon. You will probably be able to fit in about three latkes at a time.

4. Reduce the heat to medium and cook each latke for a couple of minutes on each side, until it is golden brown. (If the heat is too high the outside turns a dark brown and burns before the inside of the latke is cooked.) If you intend to freeze any latkes, cook them until only just lightly golden, because they will be cooked further when reheated.

5. Remove the latkes with a fish slice or spatula and drain off excess oil on kitchen paper. Repeat to fry the next batch, and continue until all are cooked, keeping the finished latkes warm in a single layer on a wire rack in the oven. You may have to increase or reduce the heat under the frying pan, especially for the subsequent batches, to get an even colour without scorching the latkes.

6. While the latkes are frying, if you're serving poached eggs, add a big pinch of salt to the boiling water in the saucepan. Crack an egg into a small cup and add a drop of vinegar. Stir the water with a balloon whisk until you get a whirlpool in the pan. Lower the cup a little into the water and slip the egg into the whirlpool. Reduce the heat to low and put a timer on for three minutes, then remove the egg with a slotted spoon and drain it on kitchen paper. Repeat to make as many eggs as you need.

7. Serve the latkes with the eggs, if using, or sour cream, chives or even smoked salmon or roast cherry tomatoes, if you're feeling flash. If you're feeling especially bling, serve all of them. A grind of pepper over the top is good here.

Packed Lunch

Top ten!

- **Great balls of broccoli**
- **Golden wonder**
- **Cheese, tomato and thyme muffins**
- **Wrap and roll**
- **Houmous and home-made tortilla chips**
- **Tuna melt parcels**
- **Sticky Chinese chicken strips**
- **Cheat's tandoori chicken**
- **Malt loaf**
- **Lunch box bars**

We would love to say that making packed lunches is our favourite part of being a parent and a joyous start to the day. But, well, we'd be lying. Truth is never in short supply around these parts and we all know they are a colossal chore.

It is a timing thing. You've just woken up with bed-head, there's breakfast to be made, children to be taken to school, jobs to go to. The last thing on your mind is buttering bread.

But don't despair; there is an easier way. At the risk of sounding like a scout, it really is all about being prepared.

Bar the sandwiches, make everything the night before. You'll thank your kind, organised self in the morning. The lunch box(es) should be hunted down, decontaminated and packed with fruit, a drink, a yogurt and biscuits… or whatever you choose.

This just leaves sandwiches to be made on the day. The fresher they are, the better they taste and thus the more likely they are to be eaten. It's not rocket science.

If you have to make sandwiches the night before, butter the bread right up to the edges and ensure that wetter ingredients – such as tomatoes – aren't placed directly next to the bread, as it makes it soggy. Grated carrots or shredded lettuce are a good alternative.

When we were growing up, the most popular sandwich fillings were meat paste (exactly what meat was unclear) or cheese. Ham, if you were posh. Children these days don't know how lucky they are! On a school trip recently we spotted tuna and cucumber, cheese and pesto and smoked salmon with cream cheese. Blimey.

Don't just limit yourself to sliced bread, either. Wraps are brilliant and there is a DIY element to them that children (OK, and adults) love. Also try pitta breads, mini rolls or bagels.

Variety is the spice of life, or so they say, so, instead of sandwiches, try dips and breadsticks, chicken bits, cheese and crackers, vegetable fritters or salads made from last night's leftover rice or pasta.

Some of the Mumsnetters' more snazzy recommendations include edamame beans straight from the pod, Tupperware pots filled with chopped fruit (spritzed with lemon juice to prevent browning) and bulk-baking flapjacks on a Sunday to last the week.

Your children may want to drink something fizzy that begins with a C, but we all know that will rot their teeth and possibly their brains. The free stuff that comes out of the tap is both cheaper and healthier. You can make water more palatable (well, you can try) by buying a re-usable water bottle and adding some lemon or lime juice.

Just as with any other area of child development, there are many different phases to packed lunches. Little ones will tend to eat what you give them but, as they get older, they may not want to stand out from their peers and will refuse to eat the delicious – but smelly – boiled eggs that were once a favourite. And, just as with any other area of child development, our advice is to roll with it. You want them to enjoy their food and feel comfortable, so listen to their requests and see if you can compromise. Otherwise you'll risk the packed lunch being binned in favour of the vending machine or chip shop.

And if all your good plans end up falling by the wayside, don't fret. There have been no recorded cases of children dying from eating cheese sandwiches and salt-and-vinegar crisps for five days on the trot.

Great balls of broccoli

**Makes 8–10 balls
(depending on size)**

1 large head of broccoli
2 eggs, lightly beaten
2 garlic cloves, crushed
Salt and pepper
Large handful of dry
  breadcrumbs
Flavourless oil, such as
  groundnut or vegetable,
  to fry

❦ Vegetarian

♥ The health bit
Broccoli is a superhero of a
vegetable. It is stuffed with
vitamin C (which helps to
boost your immune system)
and folic acid. And just two
broccoli florets count as one
of your five-a-day.

Suspend your disbelief, because this recipe could make your
children like broccoli. Grating it – instead of serving florets whole
– makes it seem somehow less threatening. Mix it with egg, garlic,
breadcrumbs, salt and pepper, mould it into balls and it becomes
a delicious fritter.

These are delicious hot or cold. Particularly when dipped
in ketchup. Ahem.

1. Wash the broccoli thoroughly. Dry it, then coarsely grate it on a cheese
grater, stalk and all.

2. Mix the grated broccoli with the eggs, then stir in the garlic thoroughly,
adding some salt and pepper, too. Mix in two-thirds of the breadcrumbs,
placing the remaining crumbs on a broad, shallow dish.

3. Form small balls of the broccoli mixture, each about the size of a
walnut. Make sure they are not too moist or they won't hold together
when you fry them. If they are, just squeeze out the excess juice in
your hands.

4. Roll each ball in the leftover breadcrumbs.

5. Pour about 5cm of oil into a deep saucepan and heat it, so that it
splutters when you throw in a couple of breadcrumbs. If you have
a deep-fat fryer, then use that. Whatever you use, *be very careful*, do not
leave the pan unattended and, if using a saucepan, make sure the oil
comes no more than one-third of the way up the sides.

6. Carefully lower some of the balls into the hot oil, using a slotted
spoon. Do not crowd the pan or the temperature of the oil will drop,
resulting in greasy fritters. Cook, turning once, until they are golden
brown all over.

7. Remove the balls with the slotted spoon and drain on kitchen
paper. Repeat to cook all the balls. You may have to adjust the heat,
so the balls cook through to the centre before they burn on the
outside. Eat hot or cold.

Golden wonder

Serves 4 adults

Unsalted butter, for
 greasing the dish
2 large courgettes (375g
 total weight), grated
3 rashers of
 bacon, chopped
1 large onion, chopped
140g self-raising flour
115ml flavourless oil,
 such as vegetable oil
5 eggs, lightly beaten
80g cheese, grated
 (whatever you prefer,
 or have in the fridge)
1 tsp thyme leaves
Pepper

♥ **The health bit**
Some people worry about
the cholesterol in eggs but
there's really no need, as it
doesn't have any impact
on cholesterol in the blood.
In fact, unless you have
been diagnosed with high
cholesterol levels, there's no
need to limit the number
of eggs you eat.

The alchemy of the oven. A few unexciting ingredients are thrown together, slowly baked and... huzzah! A delicious packed lunch awaits. You may not be convinced when you read through this recipe: onions and bacon just thrown in, without browning or caramelising? Grated courgettes? Sigh. But trust us. This is a lunch to be proud of. Cut it open and a fluffy omelette-style cake awaits! The French have been making savoury 'cakes' for years, and with good reason. So go on, just try it.

This goes very well with a green salad and a glass of red wine for grown ups. Make it in the evening, have half for your supper and (try to remember to) save some for the kids' lunch. You can bake this mixture in muffin cases if you prefer, for maximum lunch box appeal; they'll take 30 minutes in the oven and you'll get about 18.

1. Preheat the oven to 180°C/fan 160°C/gas mark 4. Lightly butter a round ovenproof dish, about 20cm in diameter.

2. In a large bowl, mix the courgettes with the bacon, onion, flour, oil, eggs, cheese and thyme, until the flour has been incorporated without any lumps. Season well with a hearty grind of black pepper.

3. Pour the mixture into the prepared dish and bake in the oven until golden on top. This will take about 50 minutes.

4. Remove from the oven and serve. Or place the dish on a wire rack and wait until it has cooled, then slice into wedges each day to parcel out for lunches.

Cheese, tomato and thyme muffins

Makes 12

200g self-raising flour

125g mature Cheddar or other hard cheese, grated

60g sun-blushed tomatoes, finely chopped

1 tsp sweet paprika

1 tsp thyme leaves

Salt

200ml milk

1 egg

A little Parmesan, or other hard cheese

☛ **You will need**

12 fairy cake cases (muffin cases make these a little too big for young children); fairy cake tray.

❦ **Vegetarian**

✳ **Freezable**

Cool the muffins completely after cooking. Open-freeze in a single layer, then transfer to a freezer bag for storage.

You'd climb mountains for your children and swim through shark-infested waters. But would you give them your last cheese, tomato and thyme muffin? Be strong. Take a deep breath and pop one in their lunch box.

If you're making a batch of these to serve throughout the week, store them in the freezer. That way, by Thursday they won't be soggy or stale. Just take the muffins out of the freezer the night before you need them and they will thaw by morning, in time to butter them and stick a filling inside. Alternatively, keep them in a paper bag and see if that works (success depends on how hot and/or humid your kitchen is).

These are delicious on their own, especially warm and buttered, but, for a more substantial lunch, just break them in half and fill with thin slices of tomato or chunks of cheese and some pickle. The ravening hordes (aka older children) might like a flask of soup to go with them.

1. Preheat the oven to 200°C/fan 180°C/gas mark 6 and place 12 fairy cake cases in a fairy cake tray.

2. Put the flour, cheese, tomatoes, paprika, thyme and ½ tsp of salt into a mixing bowl and stir. Measure the milk in a jug, then crack the egg into it and give it a good mix. Stir this into the dry ingredients gradually, while stirring, until all is combined together, but don't overdo it.

3. Spoon the batter into the cake cases, then grate the Parmesan cheese over the top. Pop in the hot oven for 15 minutes, but keep an eye on them towards the end; you want the tops to be browned but not scorched.

4. Take out of the oven and cool on a wire rack.

Wrap and roll

Makes 1

Smear of mayonnaise,
  or well softened
  unsalted butter
1 wrap or flour tortilla
1 small carrot, grated
Handful of grated cheese
Small handful of raisins
Cucumber batons

For a smoked salmon wrap
Lashings of cream cheese
Slices of smoked salmon

For a ham, mozzarella and pesto wrap
Slathering of pesto
Handful of grated
  mozzarella
Slice of ham

For a jewelled rice wrap
Well softened butter,
  cream cheese, or pesto
Handful of cold rice
Scattering of finely
  chopped carrot
Scattering of finely
  chopped cucumber
Scattering of finely
  chopped red pepper

❦ Vegetarian
Not the smoked salmon one!

♥ The health bit
Go the wholesome hog and
use wholemeal wraps.

Wraps are now a firm part of every child's lunch box vernacular. And quite right, too. They make sliced bread – with its unloved crusts and soggy ways – seem like a poor relation. Children love assembling their own and you're well within your rights to send them to school with a couple of wraps, a pot of houmous and some grated cheese. However, if you want something that is stuffed with veggies, wouldn't look out of place at a posh garden party, but takes minimal effort, then here we show you how to Wrap and Roll (™Mumsnet).

1. Spread the mayonnaise or butter all over the wrap, right to the very edges (this will help it to stick when you come to roll it).

2. Sprinkle the carrot, cheese and raisins all over and pop the cucumber batons in the middle.

3. Roll up the wrap, tucking in the sides as you go. When rolled completely, slice it on the diagonal.

Other ideas
Obviously this is just one way you can wrap and roll. You could use cream cheese with smoked salmon, or pesto with mozzarella and ham. (Use the cream cheese or pesto in the same way as the mayonnaise or butter, above, to help the wrap stick.)

For a jewelled rice wrap, spread the butter, cream cheese or pesto all over the wrap, as before. Mix the rice, carrot, cucumber and red pepper and use it to fill the wrap. Beware: this filling has a dangerous tendency to fall out, but the tighter you wrap it, the less likely that is to happen.

Houmous and home-made tortilla chips

For the houmous
400g tin of chickpeas,
   drained and rinsed
1 garlic clove, crushed
3 tbsp tahini
2 tbsp olive oil, plus more
   to serve (optional)
Juice of ½ lemon
Salt and pepper

For the tortilla chips
4 wraps or flour tortillas
A little olive oil

♥ Vegetarian

✳ Freezable
The houmous part is, anyway.

♥ **The health bit**
Shop-bought houmous is
often very salty. But when
you make it yourself, you are
in control of the salt cellar.
Remember, a little extra
lemon juice can often do the
same job as adding more salt.
Honest. Just try it.

This is the all-else-fails, ultimate fast food snack/lunch/dinner where we come from. Children seem to love it and we are not complaining, because it is good for them. It used to be one of those things – like ketchup – that there was no point in making, because the shop-bought stuff was so good. Well, no more. This is the ultimate houmous recipe. It is fast (whizzing a tin of chickpeas in a food processor), easy and cheap.

It works perfectly with these home-made tortilla chips or, of course, with pitta bread, bread sticks or cucumber sticks.

1. For the houmous, whizz together the ingredients with 2 tbsp of water using a food processor or hand-held blender. When smooth, season to taste. That is it. Really. Serve in a dish, or individual pots with a little oil and/or pepper sprinkled over, if you like.

2. To make the tortilla chips, preheat the oven to 180°C/fan 160°C/gas mark 4. Cut the wraps into triangles with a pair of scissors (as if you were cutting a pizza). Brush both sides of each slice with olive oil and place on a baking tray lined with greaseproof paper. Bake for about five minutes, until they turn golden, watching that they don't scorch.

3. Remove the tortilla chips from the oven and place on a wire rack; they will crisp up as they cool. Before serving, sprinkle with a little salt, if you want.

Tuna melt parcels

Makes 4 large parcels

185g tin of tuna, drained
1 roasted red pepper
  (from a jar), deseeded
  and chopped
100g Cheddar or other
  hard cheese, grated
200g tin of sweetcorn,
  drained and rinsed
Salt and pepper
500g pack of puff pastry
Plain flour, to dust
Milk, to brush

❋ Freezable
Cool the parcels completely
after cooking. Open-freeze in
a single layer, then transfer to
freezer bags for storage.

♥ The health bit
Crank up these parcels' health
benefits by using tuna tinned
in oil or spring water, instead
of in salty brine. Or swap the
tuna for super-healthy tinned
salmon instead, for even
more of those omega-3
heart-boosting fatty acids.

Sometimes sarnies seem like the easy option for packed lunches. Bread, butter, plus a random filling from the fridge. These parcels are similarly easy – roll pastry, fill with bits and bobs from the fridge, bake – but feel a bit more impressive. It's very little extra effort, but you get a whole different level of kudos. Make these when you think someone's looking.

1. Preheat the oven to 200°C/fan 180°C/gas mark 6. Line a baking tray with greaseproof paper.

2. Place the tuna in a bowl and thoroughly flake it with a fork. Mix in the pepper, cheese and sweetcorn and season to taste.

3. Roll out the pastry on a lightly floured surface to a 35cm square about as thick as a pound coin. Cut into four squares.

4. Spread a dollop of one-quarter of the tuna mixture over a diagonal half of each square, leaving a border of about 1.5cm. Dampen the edges of the pastry with water and fold over the other (empty) diagonal half, to make triangular parcels. Pinch the edges to seal them, or press down with a fork.

5. Brush the top of each parcel with milk (this will help it brown) and place on the prepared baking tray. Bake in the oven for 25 minutes, or until golden.

6. Remove the parcels from the oven and allow to cool on a wire rack, or season and eat while still warm.

Sticky Chinese chicken strips

Serves 1 adult

Small piece of root ginger, finely grated
1 garlic clove, crushed
1 tbsp soy sauce
1 tbsp runny honey
1 skinless boneless chicken breast, cut into strips
Sesame oil (or sunflower if you can't find sesame)

✻ Freezable
Ideally, freeze the marinated chicken before cooking (as long as the chicken was not previously frozen). If freezing it after cooking, make up and add an extra spoonful of marinade to the bag, to prevent the chicken drying out in the freezer.

These are almost too good to be true. They are certainly almost too good to give to the children for packed lunch. OK, they take longer to make than a humble ham sandwich, but put these in your child's lunch box and you can be 100 per cent sure they will be scoffed in seconds. Marinating the chicken needn't be fiddly, especially if you use frozen chopped garlic and ginger (available at most big supermarkets). The beauty of this dish is that you can make it the night before, pop it in some Tupperware and eat it, cold, the next day. (It's not suitable for babies less than one year old, because of the honey in the sauce, see page 14.)

If you want something more substantial, toss the sticky chicken through some noodles or rice with peas and sweetcorn.

1. Put the ginger, garlic, soy sauce and honey in a non-metallic shallow bowl and add the chicken strips. Toss until they are thoroughly coated in the marinade, then cover and leave in the fridge for at least eight hours (if you are feeling terribly organised, make a larger batch, divide it into little bags and freeze them at this stage).

2. The next day, shake off the excess marinade and fry the chicken in the sesame oil. When it is brown, add the remaining marinade from the bowl. Cook, stirring occasionally, until the chicken strips turn a golden colour and are sticky and cooked through. Cut through one of the thicker chicken strips to check; there should be no trace of pink. If there is, cook for a minute longer, then check again.

3. Serve with the sauce. And pack a napkin.

Cheat's tandoori chicken

Serves 4 adults, plus leftovers (or fewer adults and more leftovers)

For the chicken
1 chicken
150ml natural yogurt
150ml mild Indian red-coloured curry paste
Juice of ½ lemon
Salt

For the spiced yogurt (optional)
3 tbsp natural yogurt
2 tsp mango chutney
1 tsp turmeric

To serve as a packed lunch
Soft flour tortillas, wraps or pitta breads
Shredded lettuce

Obviously, mixing your own spice blend is high on the priority list for most parents. Alongside ironing sheets, there are few things more important. However, sometimes you have to let go. Uncurl those fingers from that pestle. Instead, buy a lovely shop-bought mild curry paste, whack it over a chicken and you've got dinner and several packed lunches' worth of sarnies taken care of. Result.

1. With a sharp knife, prick the chicken all over. Mix the yogurt, curry paste, lemon juice and salt to taste in a bowl. Rub the marinade all over the chicken, as well as under the skin of the breast. Put on a plate, cover and place in the fridge to marinate for as long as you've got; overnight would be perfect.

2. Take the chicken out of the fridge to return to room temperature while you preheat the oven to 200°C/fan 180°C/gas mark 6.

3. Place the chicken in a roasting tin and cover with foil. Cook in the oven for 20 minutes per 500g, plus 20 minutes more. Halfway through, baste the chicken with any remaining marinade. When the chicken has cooked for two-thirds of the total time, remove the foil so it will brown.

4. Meanwhile, make the spiced yogurt, if you want (it's good!), by combining all the ingredients in a bowl and mixing.

5. Once the chicken has had its cooking time, remove it from the oven and pull a leg away from the body. Skewer it here; the juices should run clear. If you see any trace of pink, put it back in the oven for another five minutes and then check again. Repeat if necessary. The skin will be darkly burnished from the curry paste, as in the photograph, right.

6. Let the chicken rest for 20 minutes, then have some for supper with the spiced yogurt and some rice. Shred the remaining meat for packed lunches, serving it in tortillas, wraps or pitta breads with the spiced yogurt and lettuce.

Malt loaf

Makes 1 small loaf

1 teacup brown sugar

1 teacup mixed fruit
  (anything you've got:
  raisins, glacé cherries,
  sultanas, apricots...)

1 teacup milk

1 teacup bran flakes

Unsalted butter, for
  greasing the tin

1 teacup self-raising flour

☛ **You will need**

1-litre loaf tin.

❦ **Vegetarian**

❄ **Freezable**

This is glorious. Straight from the oven, the fruit gooey and caramelised, a large wedge slathered in butter can improve absolutely any time of day. And there's the crux of the problem: delicious cake + no willpower = crumbs for kids' lunch boxes. Fortunately this cake is so easy that, with a teacup of this and a teacup of that, you can quickly knock it up again, if greed gets the better of you.

1. Pour the sugar, fruit, milk and bran flakes into a large mixing bowl, stir, cover and leave for one hour.

2. When you're ready to bake the malt loaf, preheat the oven to 180°C/fan 160°C/gas mark 4 and lightly butter a one-litre loaf tin.

3. Add the self-raising flour to the cake mix and stir well. Pour into the loaf tin and bake for 50 minutes, or until a sharp knife or skewer inserted into the centre comes out clean.

4. Let the loaf cool for about 15 minutes before slicing and devouring. You can store this in a tin for up to a week, but, if it feels a bit dry, why not toast it and/or slather in butter?

Lunch box bars

Makes 10

100g unsalted butter,
  plus more for the tin
200g porridge oats
200g mixed seeds
3 tbsp honey
100g light brown sugar
100g dried fruit, chopped
  into bits if large
  (anything you've got:
  raisins, glacé cherries,
  sultanas, apricots...)
1 tsp ground cinnamon
  (optional)

☞ **You will need**
18 x 25cm tray-bake tin.

❦ **Vegetarian**

❄ **Freezable**
Cool the bars completely after
cooking. Open-freeze in a
single layer, then transfer to
a freezer bag for storage.

♥ **The health bit**
Sweet though these may be,
they are healthier than plain
flapjacks because of the seeds
and dried fruits. Nonetheless,
you might want to keep slices
relatively small.

Are children's chocolate bars getting smaller these days? Maybe we are just getting bigger. Perhaps the two things are even related... But if you want to give your child something more sustaining in their packed lunch, these are a godsend. Easy to make, and even the fussiest child will like them. The ingredients list is flexible and can be adapted to your child's taste; you can substitute desiccated coconut or nuts for some or all of the weight of the seeds. Don't serve these to babies less than one year old, because of the honey (see page 14).

1. Preheat the oven to 160°C/fan 140°C/gas mark 3. Butter an 18 x 25cm shallow tray-bake tin and line the base with greaseproof paper.

2. Toast the oats and seeds, separately, in a baking tray in the oven until lightly brown; this will take five to 10 minutes. Watch them carefully, as they burn quickly.

3. Warm the 100g of butter, the honey and sugar gently in a saucepan. Don't let it boil, or it will become like glue.

4. Add the toasted oats and seeds and the dried fruit, plus the cinnamon, if you like it, to the saucepan. Mix until everything is nicely coated.

5. Tip into the tin, press down lightly and bake for 30 minutes.

6. Allow the bake to cool in the tin before you slice it into 10 bars, otherwise they will crumble.

Soup

Top ten!

- **A simple vegetable soup**
- **Frog soup**
- **Leek, potato and ham soup**
- **The unlikely lads: broccoli and mushroom soup**
- **Sunny sweetcorn soup**
- **The vitamin injection**
- **Sweet potato soup**
- **Butternut and red onion soup**
- **Minestrone**
- **Speedy chicken noodle soup**

Warm, comforting, quick to knock up and cheap, soup's list of achievements doesn't stop there – it's also healthy. After a busy weekend where the nutritional highlight is a bag of Pom-bears and a banana, or when a motorway stop-off for pre-packed muffins (they've got fruit in them!) feels healthy, your five-a-day can seem like a distant dream. That's where soup comes in. It's like money in the bank. Jam-packed with vitamins, one bowl can provide two, even three of your five portions of fruit and vegetables a day. Have a bowl for lunch before you go away, then mainline soup when you get back and your body won't even notice the weekend's nutritional blip. Add some beans or pulses for extra fibre and protein and you and yours will go to nutritional nirvana.

Plus, kids tend to like it. Obviously no one has told them that soup is just vegetables whizzed up, so keep it under your hat. In the meantime, sneak in as many different types of vegetable as you think you can get away with. Certain things (think sweet potatoes) mean you can mess around with the other ingredients, as their sweetness is a good foil for more challenging vegetables.

And it doesn't have to be just vegetables. If your children need a little more persuading, chorizo, cheese and bacon can make the most worthy soup into a pretty appealing bowlful. If you use these as seasoning rather than as the main event, the soup even maintains its nutritional value. Sprinkle a little cheese or some crumbled bacon on top and elevate your soup to something more than puréed veg, which brings us on to garnish…

Think of garnish as a chance to soup up your soup, to add a different layer of flavours. Any herbs sprinkled over the top will make it deliciously different: chives, basil, a fried sage leaf… Stir in a swirl of yogurt, grate in some lemon zest or add a sprinkle of sweet smoked paprika. All these flavours can send your soup soaring, turning a Monday night stalwart into something altogether more exciting.

Soup is generally low in fat too. Unless you lace it with butter, that is. Or coconut milk (yep, we're guilty). But that fat can be worth it, if it means your child is eating vitamins that they otherwise wouldn't.

We hope the soups in this chapter will broaden your repertoire. There may be some which become family favourites. And the thing about soup is that you can adapt, be adventurous, dump one ingredient, insert another. Mushroom and broccoli doesn't float your boat? Then drop the offending ingredient and swap in something else.

As long as you make it yourself, everything else about soup is flexible. There are many things that are just as good bought as they are home-made (we're looking at you, pasta), but soup isn't among them. Shop-bought soup can be high in salt and is likely to have fewer nutrients than soup you make at home. It's also more expensive.

A fundamental soup ingredient is stock. Normally we've always got a stock pot bubbling away in the background, full of aromatic herbs – from the garden, of course – and some fennel fronds. But on the rare occasion (*cough*) that there isn't, we use the bought stuff. However, to stop all our soups tasting the same (basically, of shop-bought stock) we dilute it and make it to half strength.

Another great thing about soup is that it freezes brilliantly. Wait for it to cool and pour individual servings into freezer bags so you can defrost exactly what you need when you need it. How smug will you feel after you've done that? Yup, it's not just the heat of the soup that is making you glow.

A simple vegetable soup

Serves 6 adults

2 carrots, sliced
1 onion, chopped
1 leek, sliced
2 celery sticks, sliced
60g red lentils
1 vegetable stock cube or
  1 tsp bouillon powder
White pepper
Chopped parsley leaves,
  to serve (optional)

❦ Vegetarian

❄ Freezable

♥ **The health bit**

Can it be possible to increase the nutritional goodness of vegetable soup? Yes! And it's so easy. Just add a tin of beans or some pulses, such as the lentils used here, and you've seriously boosted its protein and fibre.

Poor old onion, celery and carrots. Stalwarts of stews; backbones of bologneses; always the bridesmaid, never the bride. Until now. Here they steal the show, in a bowl that celebrates the simple and the delicate, elbowing out those seasonal vegetables with their showy flavours and their fleeting harvests. Just don't forget the white pepper, it transforms this soup. If you fancy a change, or have some other vegetables to use up, stick them in! Squash, parsnips or sweet potato would all work well.

1. Fill a large saucepan that has a lid with two litres of water. Pop its lid on and put it on to boil.

2. While you're waiting, prepare and chop the vegetables.

3. Once the water has boiled, add in the vegetables. Stir in the lentils and crumbled vegetable stock cube or bouillon powder. Sprinkle some white pepper to taste into the mix and stir. Return to the boil, then cover, reduce the heat to a simmer and cook for one hour.

4. Purée the soup with a hand-held blender (by far the easiest way, this also means less washing up than a standing blender or food processor). Or leave it chunky, if you are in a more rugged mood. Or blend just half of it, if you're feeling indecisive. Scatter with parsley, if you want, and make sure there are big hunks of white bread and butter on the table.

Frog soup

Serves 4 adults

Glug of olive oil
1 leek, finely sliced
1 celery stick, chopped
1 large potato (about 225g),
    finely chopped
1 litre vegetable stock
280g frozen petits pois
    or peas
Salt and pepper
Grated cheese (whatever
    you prefer, or have in the
    fridge) and/or crème
    fraîche, to serve

❦ Vegetarian

❄ Freezable

♥ The health bit
Peas may be small but, for
their size, they're a brilliant
source of vitamin C, which
helps with a healthy immune
system. These tiny little
wonder-foods also provide
useful amounts of vitamins
B1 and B6 (good for a healthy
heart and nervous system and
for making red blood cells),
and are rich in folic acid and
also soluble fibre, which helps
to control cholesterol.

This is a dish that we didn't name, but don't let the title put you off. It is made from peas and we think it gets its moniker from the fluorescent green colour. If you want to snazz it up, add a small handful of mint leaves with the peas. Anyway, it is lovely: tasty, healthy and guaranteed to give you a spring in your step. So hop to it. Make some. It is unfrog-ettable.

1. Heat the oil in a large saucepan that has a lid over a medium heat. Add the leek and fry for five minutes until softened.

2. Add the celery and potato and cook for a further five minutes.

3. Pour the stock over the vegetables and bring to the boil. Cover, reduce the heat and simmer for 15 minutes.

4. Check the potato is tender, then add the petits pois or peas and simmer for five more minutes.

5. Using a hand-held blender, blend the soup until smooth, then season to taste.

6. Top with some grated cheese or a swirl of crème fraîche, or both, and grind some pepper over if you like.

Leek, potato and ham soup

Serves 4 adults

Glug of olive oil
1 onion, chopped
1 garlic clove, crushed
4 leeks, sliced
3 baking-type potatoes
(about 600g in total),
finely chopped
1.4 litres hot vegetable
or chicken stock
Salt and pepper
3 thick slices of ham,
finely chopped
Dash of cream, to serve
(optional)

❄ Freezable

♥ **The health bit**

Leeks, in addition to tasting lovely, also happen to be an excellent source of vitamin B6, good for making healthy blood cells and boosting your immune system.

If you thought leek and potato soup was a classic that could not be improved upon, even one tiny slurpy bit, then you were wrong. Adding some chopped ham to a national favourite is a touch of genius. It is an obvious combo and turns this soup into something altogether more hearty and perfect for when it is cold outside. The jury is out on how to serve it. Some like theirs whizzed in a blender to a pale green velvety purée, like the French vichyssoise. Others prefer more of a clear broth with vegetables bobbing around. You can sit on the fence and do half and half. But bread and butter are obligatory. A swirl of cream looks nice, too.

1. Heat the olive oil in a saucepan that has a lid over a medium heat, then gently fry the onion and garlic for about a minute.

2. Add the leeks and potatoes. Give it all a good stir and reduce the heat, allowing everything to cook gently for about five minutes. Make sure the leeks don't go too brown; burnt leeks are bitter leeks.

3. When the onions and leeks are soft and cooked through, add the stock. Bring the soup to the boil, then reduce the heat, cover and simmer for 20 minutes, or until the potatoes are tender. Season to taste.

4. If you want to go Frenchy Frenchy, then whizz up the mixture until it is smooth using a hand-held blender. Or whizz half, then mix it with the remaining chunky soup.

5. Add the ham at the end and stir through until it is warm. Add the cream, if using, season and serve with bread and butter.

The unlikely lads: broccoli and mushroom soup

Serves 6 adults

Knob of unsalted butter
Glug of olive oil
1 onion, chopped
2 garlic cloves, chopped
500g mushrooms, sliced
Salt and pepper
Large head of broccoli,
    chopped into florets
1.5 litres vegetable stock
Double cream, to serve
    (optional)

❦ Vegetarian

❄ Freezable
This soup can be frozen before the double cream is added.

♥ The health bit
For a lot of kids, mushrooms are the Marmite of the vegetable world. Sneaking them in via this recipe gives children a host of B vitamins including folic acid (aka vitamin B9) and vitamin B5, as well as selenium and copper. Broccoli's no slacker either; it delivers B vitamins, a slug of vitamin C and phytochemicals, believed to help protect against some cancers. Mushroom and broccoli may not be a famous double act, but they are an extremely healthy one.

Ant and Dec, country and western, salt and pepper, broccoli and mushroom... OK, we admit it may not be as famous as the other pairings, but that doesn't mean it doesn't work. Oh no. It's just that no one else has thought of it. We are trailblazers! So trust us and put these two everyday vegetables together. We promise you will get a rich and flavoursome soup that doesn't really taste of either broccoli or mushroom. Just a delicious meld of deeply savoury, umami-rich flavours that also happen to do you good.

1. Melt the butter in a large saucepan that has a lid. Add the olive oil, then fry the onion until it begins to turn translucent. The olive oil stops the butter burning, which lets you cook at a higher temperature and keeps a lovely buttery flavour. Throw in the garlic and cook for one minute.

2. Add the mushrooms, cover and cook, giving them a shake and an occasional stir, until they are browned and a bit sloppy.

3. Season with salt and pepper, then add the broccoli. Pour in enough stock to cover all the veg, plus a tiny bit more, then increase the heat.

4. Once the soup comes to the boil, reduce the heat, cover and let it simmer for about 20 minutes.

5. Take the soup off the heat and whizz it up with a hand-held blender. Serve, swirling in some double cream if you want a lovely creamy finish.

Sunny sweetcorn soup

2 tbsp unsalted butter
1 level tbsp plain flour
280ml milk
1 vegetable or chicken
  stock cube
340g tin of sweetcorn,
  drained and rinsed
5 spring onions,
  finely chopped
Salt and pepper

❧ **Vegetarian**
Use vegetable stock.

❄ **Freezable**

♥ **The health bit**
We're pro-sweetcorn because it's such a good source of soluble fibre, the stuff that helps reduce high blood cholesterol levels and balance blood sugar. It also turns out to be packed with vitamin B6, which we need to make healthy blood cells and run a strong immune system.

This is made more or less entirely from food most of us are either guaranteed to have in the cupboard or can easily get from the corner shop. The wonder of cooking is that, out of seemingly prosaic ingredients, something so delicious can be made. Kids love this. If you have some ham, or leftover cold chicken, chop it up and throw it in at the end, cooking just enough to thoroughly heat it through.

1. Melt the butter in a saucepan over a medium heat and stir in the flour until the two are combined in a gently bubbling paste.

2. Slowly stir in the milk, then gradually add the same amount of water and crumble in the stock cube. Bring to the boil, whisking occasionally to get rid of any lumps.

3. Add the sweetcorn and spring onions and simmer for two to five minutes. As if by magic, the soup will thicken up. It is meant to be quite lumpy (blame the sweetcorn) so, if you prefer a smoother soup, blitz either all of it, or half of it, with a hand–held blender until it is as creamy – or nubbly – as you desire.

4. Season and serve.

The vitamin injection

25g unsalted butter
Glug of olive oil
1 onion, chopped
1 butternut squash,
  prepared and chopped
  into cubes (see page 86)
2 sweet potatoes,
  peeled and roughly
  chopped
80g frozen spinach
80g broccoli, chopped
  into florets
400g tin of chickpeas,
  drained and rinsed
400g tin of butter beans,
  drained and rinsed
1 tsp turmeric
1.5 litres vegetable stock

To serve
1 tsp cumin seeds
Crème fraîche

❦ Vegetarian

✳ Freezable

♥ The health bit
Sneaking veggies into soup
is not all about eating *greens*.
We need an array of coloured
veg, as they have different
nutrients. Nutritionists call
this 'eating a rainbow', a
phrase you may wish to
use on any resistant kids.

Jam-packed with vegetables, this is great to make when you want to know your kids are getting enough veg. Make a big batch, pop some in the freezer and bring it out for nutritional emergencies. In this version the chickpeas and butter beans are puréed into the soup, but you might prefer to add them to the smooth soup at the end, just to heat through, for a bit of texture.

1. In a large saucepan with a lid, gently melt the butter, then add the olive oil. Throw in the onion and fry gently until it is soft and translucent.

2. Add the squash, sweet potatoes, spinach, broccoli, chickpeas and butter beans, turning to coat in the buttery juices, then add the turmeric and pour in the stock.

3. Bring to the boil, then reduce the heat, cover and simmer for 40 minutes, or until everything is nice and soft.

4. Take the soup off the heat and let it cool a little, then use a hand-held blender to purée it.

5. Dry-fry the cumin seeds in a small frying pan until they smell aromatic. If you don't want to eat whole seeds, grind them to a powder in a mortar and pestle (cumin is always far better toasted and freshly ground). Serve each bowl of soup with a dollop of crème fraîche and a sprinkling of the cumin on the top.

Sweet potato soup

Serves 4 adults

Glug of olive oil
1 large onion, chopped
3 large sweet potatoes
 (about 900g), peeled
 and chopped
1 baking-type potato
 (about 200g), chopped
750ml vegetable or
 chicken stock, plus
 more if needed
400ml tin of coconut milk

To serve
Sweet chilli sauce
 (optional)
Handful of coriander
 leaves, torn (optional)

♥ Vegetarian
Use vegetable stock.

✳ Freezable
This is best frozen before
adding coconut milk, but you
can freeze it after (just reheat
very gently, or it might split).

♥ The health bit
Sweet potatoes are a great
source of betacarotene,
an antioxidant which is
converted into vitamin A
in the body. Make sure
coconut milk is only an
occasional treat, as it's high
in saturated fats.

Sweet potatoes are the penny sweets of the vegetable world: delicious and loved by children. But, unlike gummy bears, they are bursting with vitamins. In this soup they are puréed with creamy coconut milk, making the perfect child-friendly bowlful. A glug of sweet chilli sauce at the end will appeal to any children who are undecided about chilli, but, if your kids are up for it, add chilli flakes or hot smoked paprika when you cook the onions.

1. Heat the oil in a large saucepan that has a lid, then add the onion and fry for five minutes over a medium heat until it becomes translucent.

2. Add all the potatoes, sweet and otherwise, and cover with stock. Cover and bring to the boil, then reduce the heat and let it simmer for 10–15 minutes, keeping an eye on the stock (top it up if it starts to go dry).

3. Once the potatoes are cooked and tender, take the pan off the heat and purée the soup with a hand-held blender.

4. Stir in the coconut milk, heat through gently and serve. Provide the sweet chilli sauce and coriander leaves for those who want them.

Butternut and red onion soup

Serves 4 adults

1 butternut squash
Glug of olive oil
Pepper
2–3 red onions, chopped
1 litre vegetable or
  chicken stock

Vegetarian
Use vegetable stock.

Freezable

The health bit
Nutritionally, butternut squash falls squarely into the category of superfood, providing serious amounts of betacarotene, which is converted into vitamin A in the body. Why is that A Good Thing? Well, because vitamin A helps strengthen immunity and fight off infections.

Despite looking impenetrable, butternut squash isn't that hard to get into. Just take a sharpish vegetable peeler and a knife and get to work. Alternatively, throw away the peeler and head for your local supermarket. Some sell butternut squash peeled, chopped, even frozen. Suddenly, making soup just got a whole lot easier. Try adding a little chopped sage to this after puréeing, or even a drained, rinsed tin of borlotti beans for added protein.

1. Preheat the oven to 200°C/fan 180°C/gas mark 6.

2. Using a vegetable peeler, peel the butternut squash. Cut it in half, remove the seeds with a spoon, then cut the flesh into 2cm chunks.

3. Put the squash in a baking tray, drizzle with some olive oil and crack some pepper over. Give the whole thing a stir and pop in the hot oven for 30 minutes. Pour some more olive oil into a saucepan that has a lid, place it over a medium-low heat and throw in the onions. Cook slowly until they are soft and translucent, then add the stock.

4. Take the squash out of the tray with a slotted spoon (you don't want too much oil to go in the soup) and add it to the pan. Bring it all to the boil, then reduce the heat, cover and simmer for 10 minutes.

5. With a hand-held blender, blitz the soup until smooth, then serve with chunks of crusty bread.

Minestrone

Serves 6 adults

Glug of olive oil
2 carrots, chopped
1 onion, finely chopped
2 potatoes, finely chopped
2 celery sticks, sliced
2 litres vegetable stock,
   plus more if needed
50g spaghetti, broken up
100g green cabbage,
   finely shredded
1 leek, sliced
400g tin of chopped
   tomatoes
Salt and pepper
Handful of basil
   leaves (optional)
Handful of Parmesan,
   or other cheese, grated

❦ Vegetarian
Leave out, or substitute,
the Parmesan cheese.

❋ Freezable
Leave out the pasta; add
it when reheating.

♥ The health bit
It won't be a surprise to hear
that a lot of children aren't
keen on cabbage. But they'll
often eat it in a soup. Cabbage
contains phytochemicals,
believed to help protect
against cancer, so it's worth
winning this particular battle.

There is something about this soup that sums up the best of life. It is filling, tasty, nutritious and cheap; exactly what food should be, but often isn't. Although it would be rude to have favourites in this book, this soup is one of ours.

1. Pour the olive oil into a very large saucepan that has a lid and place it over a medium heat. Fry the carrots, onion, potatoes and celery until softened but not browned.

2. Add the stock and bring to the boil, then reduce the heat, cover and simmer for 15 minutes.

3. Tip in the spaghetti, cabbage, leek and tomatoes, stirring until the soup returns to a simmer, then cover and cook for a further 15 minutes.

4. Season. For a less chunky soup, add more stock, or even water. Tear in the basil, if using, and serve with grated cheese over each bowl.

Speedy chicken noodle soup

Serves 2 hungry adults

1 litre vegetable or chicken
   stock, or miso soup
1 skinless boneless chicken
   breast, sliced into
   thin strips
1 red pepper, sliced
4 spring onions,
   finely sliced
4 mushrooms, sliced
1 carrot, grated
1 nest of dried egg noodles
2 tbsp dark soy sauce
Handful of chopped
   coriander leaves

Most children love both noodles and chicken, so this is a good entry-level bowlful for those who proclaim they don't like soup. The vegetable quotient can also be upped depending on the audience. Here we suggest red pepper, spring onion, mushroom and carrot, but sweetcorn and peas would work just as well for fussier eaters.

1. In a saucepan that has a lid, heat the stock or miso to a simmer.

2. Add the chicken carefully and cook for 10 minutes, or until cooked through. You can check this by fishing a big piece out and cutting it in half to check it is not pink in the middle; if it is, simmer for a few minutes more before checking another piece.

3. Tip in the vegetables – reserving the green parts of the spring onions – and noodles and cook for another five minutes.

4. Just before serving, add the soy sauce, reserved green spring onion bits and the coriander.

One-Pot Wonders

Top ten!

- Lettuce risotto
- Kid-friendly potato and chickpea curry
- A tart for ladies who lunch
- Salmon español
- A sophisticated sea bass
- One-pot, slightly spicy chicken
- Chicken scooter
- Pork and apple casserole
- The 'holy trinity' stew
- Lumberjack stew

We nicknamed this chapter The Holy Grail, because this is what we search for when looking for the perfect family recipe. Simple, tasty and uncomplicated meals that even those with little time or cookery skill can rustle up after work or while little people are weaving around their legs.

They are easily thrown together without poring over the recipe, visiting specialist ingredient shops or breaking into a nervous sweat. We love them and are over the moon to have found them.

But more than that, the main cause of joy is that every recipe is cooked in one pot. Yes! Really! All the veg are in there too! These recipes are the equivalent to the killer dress in your wardrobe. Fantastic on their own, they remove the need to make decisions. Which top should I wear with this skirt? Shall I do peas and oven chips? Yawn yawn. The brain-sapping everyday decisions are replaced by the knowledge that what you are serving up does the job all by itself. Just like that red dress you've got.

Carbohydrates are often – but not always – included in the main dish. When they are not, try the dish without them. Most are so full of tasty vegetables and sauces that their absence won't be noted. If that sounds like a step too far outside your comfort zone, then some simple crusty bread eaten alongside should satisfy any craving without straying too far from the idea of one-pot simplicity. This leaves you with less washing up and more time to put your feet up.

It is no surprise this is one of our favourite chapters, containing loads of recipes we cook again and again. Big love to the Mumsnetter who gave us Chicken scooter, it knocked our (pop) socks off. The lamb, butternut squash, and chickpea curry – aka The 'holy trinity' stew – is the ultimate crowd-pleasing bobby-dazzler. We wouldn't have had the courage to cook sea bass without the recipe in this chapter, where it is served with tomatoes and chilli. And the lightly spiced Kid-friendly potato and chickpea curry is as cheap to make as it is cheerful to eat.

In fact, it was a good thing that there *was* a child-friendly curry, because the Pork and apple casserole was so good it made us not want to share. The Lumberjack stew reawakened in us a need to eat the rustic, the unpretentious, the parsnips.

And then, the Lettuce risotto. Yes, we too were sceptical. But since making this dish for Mumsnet, we've become almost evangelical about the incredible flexibility of this humble salad stalwart.

Most of these dishes work for the whole family, meaning they can be eaten by your children at their tea time, then by you a couple of hours later with minimal extra effort. They are the kind of recipes that help build confidence in the kitchen. Partly because they are fail-safe; partly because they are all easy to adapt. Good cooking is as much about having the confidence to try different combinations (aka to use up what you have in the fridge) as it is about slavishly following a recipe.

Some of the recipes here are posh enough to serve to guests (Salmon español, we mean you!) and all are delicious enough to have easily made it into our regular family weekday recipe repertoire. And did we mention there is less washing up? We're smitten.

Lettuce risotto

Serves 4 adults

2–3 tbsp olive oil
1 onion, chopped
1 garlic clove,
    finely chopped
300g arborio rice
1.2 litres hot vegetable
    or chicken stock
1 large lettuce or
    2 Little Gems, leaves
    finely shredded
100g frozen peas
Salt and pepper
Parmesan, or other hard
    cheese, to serve

♥ Vegetarian
Substitute another hard
cheese for the Parmesan,
and use vegetable stock.

♥ The health bit
Darker salad leaves contain
higher levels of vitamins,
minerals and phytochemicals
than lighter leaves, so try
using kale, rocket or spinach
as an alternative to lettuce.

Lettuce and rice together? You are within your rights to feel a bit sceptical. But trust us; this is a great summer-time dish that will change the way you view lettuce. This is one time in your life when you want your leaves wilted. And yes, risotto does need constant stirring, but what's wrong with stirring? Think of it as meditation... You can use this recipe as a template; all risottos are made in the same way. Instead of lettuce, soak some dried mushrooms and add them to the rice, using their soaking liquid as part of the stock; or add chopped sage leaves and puréed butternut squash... the only limit is your imagination. And what your children will eat.

1. Heat the olive oil in a large pan and add the onion. Fry until it begins to soften, then add the garlic and continue to fry until the onion starts to turn translucent, which will take around five minutes. Add the rice and give it a stir until each grain is coated in oil.

2. Pour in a little hot stock and stir until the rice has absorbed it, then add another. Keep doing this at intervals, stirring all the time.

3. After about 15 minutes, add the lettuce and peas. Stir gently to mix together. This is the bit where it just looks wrong. Who dropped their salad in the rice? It will also seem as if you have added far too much lettuce, but it soon wilts and blends into the rice.

4. Stir in the last few ladles of stock.

5. The risotto is ready when all the stock has been absorbed, about five minutes after you've added the lettuce. The rice should be tender, but with a slight bite in the centre. Taste and season, grating in some of the Parmesan, if you want. And there you have it: a delicious, creamy risotto. Serve. And pass around more of the cheese.

Kid-friendly potato and chickpea curry

Serves 4 adults

1 tsp fennel seeds
1 tsp cumin seeds
3 tbsp vegetable oil
400g tin of chickpeas,
   drained and rinsed
2 baking-type potatoes
   (about 400g in total),
   cut into cubes
1 onion, chopped
2 garlic cloves, crushed
1 tsp turmeric
1 heaped tsp curry
   powder of your choice
   (garam masala is good)
400g tin of chopped
   tomatoes
200ml vegetable stock
Salt and pepper
1 tsp ground cinnamon
2 star anise
1 tbsp honey
100g spinach (optional)

🌱 **Vegetarian**

❄ **Freezable**

♥ **The health bit**
This dish provides two of your five-a-day. Go one step further and boost the protein levels by serving it with a raita made from yogurt mixed with chopped cucumber and mint.

A great Friday night stalwart. Forget about getting a takeaway, this is quick to put together and cheap. Don't be scared by the long-ish ingredients list, there's nothing that you won't use again. Mild and fragrant (with optional spinach) means there needn't be anything green or spicy to put children off. This tastes great the next day, so make it in advance if you can.

1. Put a saucepan that has a lid on the hob and turn the heat to medium. Then add the fennel and cumin seeds and toast them until they give off a delicious aroma.

2. Stir in the oil, then the chickpeas, potatoes, onion, garlic, turmeric and curry powder. Fry gently for a couple of minutes until the potatoes have taken on the colour of the spices.

3. Now add the tomatoes and about half the stock. Season with salt and pepper, then throw in the cinnamon and star anise and stir in the honey (use sugar instead if you are going to serve this to babies less than one year old, see page 14). Bring to a boil, then reduce the heat, cover and simmer for 45 minutes to one hour.

4. If your children like spinach (ha!), add it a minute or so before serving, let it wilt, then stir it through. Fish out the two star anise (they are far too crunchy and pungent to eat) and serve the curry with rice or naan bread and some seasoned yogurt, if you like.

A tart for ladies who lunch

Serves 4 adults

320g sheet of ready-rolled
 shortcrust pastry
Unsalted butter, for
 greasing the dish
8 asparagus spears
Salt and pepper
2 eggs
125ml double cream
Squeeze of lemon juice
1 tsp chopped
 parsley leaves
80g smoked salmon
 trimmings

☛ **You will need**
24–25cm round pie dish.

✽ **Freezable**
Cook, cool and freeze.

♥ **The health bit**
Salmon – like its fishy friends
mackerel, sardines and tuna
– is a good source of omega-3
fatty acids, which in turn are
good for your heart.

This smoked salmon and asparagus tart is perfect for impressing when mother-in-law/bosses/sons' girlfriends come over for lunch. It can be baked ahead, meaning stress-free entertaining. It looks gorgeous and is delicious with just a green salad. Our only other serving suggestion is a fork and a napkin. In company, that is. If not, we suggest fingers.

Asparagus is cheapest and tastiest during the English season (May to June). Smoked salmon trimmings – available at most large supermarkets – are cheaper than whole slices and also eliminate the need to chop. We love a shortcut.

1. Preheat the oven to 190°C/fan 170°C/gas mark 5. Take the pastry out of the fridge 30 minutes before you need it.

2. Butter or oil a 24–25cm pie dish. Drape the sheet of pastry over the dish, pressing it down lightly so it is a snug fit. Patch it if necessary and trim the edges, but leave a slight overhang, as pastry shrinks in the oven.

3. The case needs blind baking, but don't fret. It is easy. Chill the case for 10 minutes. Now, forget everything you've heard about baking beans, the pastry just needs pricking all over (and we mean all over: at least 20 or so times) with a fork, to release any air bubbles caused in baking. Cook the case for 20 minutes until golden brown all over.

4. Meanwhile, put on some water to boil and get your steamer out (if you don't have one, just boil the asparagus). To ensure you only have the tenderest spears in your tart, hold each at both ends, then bend until it snaps. Use the woody ends for soup. Place the spears in the steamer and salt lightly. Steam until tender, then drain well (they must be dry).

5. Crack the eggs into a small bowl and beat them lightly. Grab a pastry brush and dip it into the eggs, so it is liberally covered. Set the brush aside on a saucer until the next step.

6. Add the cream, lemon juice and parsley to the eggs, then the salmon, salt and pepper, and stir until it is evenly mixed. Carefully pour the mixture into the pie case (the case doesn't need to cool first), then place

the asparagus on top – evenly in a top and tail fashion or randomly –
but so the tips (the best bit) are evenly distributed. Grab your eggy pastry
brush and use it to brush the top edges of the pastry rim.

7. Pop the tart carefully into the oven and cook for 20 minutes (but check
it after 15 minutes). It will rise slightly, before sinking back down. This
tastes as good as it looks, either hot or at room temperature.

Salmon español

Serves 4 adults

2 tbsp olive oil
1 onion, chopped
400g potatoes, peeled and
  chopped into 1cm cubes
2 garlic cloves, crushed
1 tsp smoked sweet paprika
2 red peppers, chopped
200ml vegetable stock
  or water
400g tin of chopped
  tomatoes
Salt and pepper
4 salmon fillets

To serve (optional)

Handful of parsley leaves,
  roughly chopped
Lime wedges

♥ The health bit

Forget expensive fish oil
supplements and eat the real
thing instead. Salmon, or any
of the other oily fish such as
mackerel, with their super-
healthy fatty acids, should
make an appearance at least
once a week in your diet.

Kids love this and so do their parents. It's wholesome, hearty and healthy. It takes 10 minutes to prepare, you can make it for the children's tea and it *still* tastes delicious a few hours later for your supper. That's one bit of prep for two delicious dinners.

1. Put the oil in a large pan or pot that has a lid and place over a medium-low heat. Add the onion and potatoes and fry for five minutes, until the onion is translucent.

2. Add the garlic, smoked paprika, red peppers, stock or water and the tomatoes and bring to the boil, then reduce the heat and let it simmer for five minutes.

3. Season, then place the salmon, skin-side up, on top of the sauce. Cover the pot and simmer for eight to 10 minutes. Remove the lid and carefully turn the salmon fillets skin-side down.

4. Scatter with parsley and serve with lime wedges, if you like.

To serve kids first and adults later

Once the broth has simmered for five minutes (at the end of step 2), spoon out and set aside what you will need for your supper later on. Then continue to cook the kids' salmon as specified in the main recipe, using only as many fillets as they will need and adding the parsley and lime wedges, if using, to their plates, rather than to the pot.

When you are ready to eat your supper, reheat the reserved broth and, once it is simmering, place your reserved salmon fillets on it. Continue as in the main recipe and season to serve.

A sophisticated sea bass

Serves 4 adults

2 large ripe tomatoes
6 tbsp olive oil
2 garlic cloves, crushed
2 tbsp finely chopped
   parsley leaves (optional)
1 tsp dried chilli flakes or
   1 fresh chilli, chopped
125ml white wine
Salt and pepper
4 sea bass fillets,
   fresh or frozen

♥ **The health bit**
White fish is high in protein
and full of vitamin B12 which
helps maintain a healthy
immune system. It's also
low in fat, which makes it
an all-round Good Thing.

This really is a dinner winner. Start cooking at 7.30pm and you'll be sitting down at the table by 7.45pm. Super-fast, no washing up and special enough to serve to friends. OK, there is a tiny bit of washing up – a frying pan and lid – but that's it.

To make this dish for children, moderate the amount of chilli (don't worry about the booze; the alcohol in the wine should burn off while it's simmering). If fresh sea bass is too expensive, check out the freezer aisle of your supermarket as frozen fillets can be quite reasonable. Serve with a hearty salad of sliced courgettes, olives and rocket, or of watercress and spring onions, and some crusty buttered bread.

1. You need to skin the tomatoes. We *know*. What a faff. But the rest of the recipe is so simple it's worth it, so stick with us. Put the tomatoes in a bowl filled with boiling water. Leave for 10 seconds, drain, then slip off the skins. Cut the tomatoes in half, scoop out and discard the seeds, then chop the flesh.

2. Heat the oil in a large frying pan that has a lid. Then add the garlic, parsley (if using) and chilli and cook for two minutes.

3. Add the tomatoes and cook for another two minutes before adding the wine. Increase the heat and bring the sauce to a simmer for a couple of minutes.

4. Season, reduce the heat and place the sea bass fillets, skin-side up, in the pan. Cover the pan and cook for five minutes, or 10 if you're using frozen fish.

5. Serve the fillets, skin-side down, with the sauce spooned over the top and seasoned to taste.

One-pot, slightly spicy chicken

Serves 4 adults

2 tbsp olive oil

2 garlic cloves, crushed

2.5cm piece of root
ginger, grated

1 tsp curry powder

3 skinless boneless chicken
breasts, each chopped
into 4

6 rashers of
bacon, chopped

1 leek, sliced

170g basmati rice

340ml hot vegetable
or chicken stock,
plus more if needed

Salt and pepper

110g frozen peas

✳ Freezable

♥ **The health bit**
Who knew that some rices
were better than others?
Not us, but apparently
basmati rice has a lower
glycaemic index than regular
long-grain white rice, so it
keeps you fuller for longer.

This is a firm family favourite; everyone loves chicken, rice and peas. Here, they are cooked with curry powder and ginger, which gives the dish a mild kick. It's a great way to introduce new flavours to little – or indeed big – people. The star quality of this recipe is the low-effort-to-high-reward ratio and, as rice and peas are already in it, there is no need to serve it with anything else. It's a midweek classic.

1. Heat the oil in a large saucepan that has a lid and add the garlic, ginger and curry powder. Cook for one minute over a medium heat, stirring. Add the chicken pieces and cook for four minutes on each side.

2. Add the bacon and leek to the pan and cook for two minutes, stirring all the time. Add the rice and give it a good stir to coat in the flavourings, then add the stock. Stir occasionally as you bring it to the boil.

3. Pop a lid on, reduce the heat and simmer the dish for 20 minutes, adding more stock if the rice dries out. Season to taste.

4. Tip in the peas and cook for a further five minutes until they are warmed through.

5. Yippee-dee-doo-dah. Dinner for four. And not a hair out of place.

Chicken scooter

Serves 4 adults

2 red onions
2 red peppers
2 aubergines
2 x 250g punnets of
   cherry tomatoes
5 garlic cloves, unpeeled
4 skinless boneless
   chicken breasts
Good glug of olive oil
Salt and pepper
300g crème fraîche

✳ **Freezable**
This is best frozen before
the crème fraîche has been
added. If you are freezing it
afterwards, reheat very gently,
or it could split.

No, we're not sure why this is called chicken scooter either. It conjures up an image of a helmet-clad hen zipping around on a moped in a leather biker jacket. Nonetheless, it is a guaranteed plate-clearer, can be rustled up quickly, contains loads of gorgeous vegetables and there is very little washing up. Win. Win. Win. Win.

1. Preheat the oven to 180°C/fan 160°C/gas mark 4.

2. Chop the vegetables into bite-sized pieces and halve any larger tomatoes. Put them in a roasting tin – one that you can use on the hob as well as in the oven – with the garlic and place the chicken on top. Drizzle with oil and season with salt and pepper.

3. Roast in the oven until the chicken is cooked through and the vegetables are soft and slightly charred (about 40 minutes).

4. Check if the chicken is cooked through by inserting a knife through the thickest part. If the juices run clear, it is ready. If there is any trace of pink, cook for a couple of minutes more and test again. Remove the chicken to a warmed plate with a slotted spoon.

5. Now tip the crème fraîche into the roasting tin, stirring over a low heat. You should be left with a gorgeous tomatoey, creamy sauce that begs 'Eat me, eat me'. It would be rude not to. Season and serve the chicken sliced, on top of the sauce, with crusty bread if you must, but the sauce is a meal in itself and no carbs are necessary. Eat with a green salad, if you like.

Pork and apple casserole

Serves 4 adults

Glug of olive oil
4 pork steaks
1 onion, finely chopped
3 rashers of streaky bacon,
    finely chopped
1 large carrot, sliced
150g (a handful of)
    mushrooms, sliced
1 cooking apple, unpeeled,
    cored and chopped
200ml cider (optional but,
    if not using, add another
    200ml stock)
450ml chicken stock
Pepper, to taste
1–2 sage leaves, chopped,
    plus more to serve
    (optional)
1 tbsp crème fraîche

✳ **Freezable**

♥ **The health bit**

Not only is pork shoulder just four per cent fat, it also contains the mineral selenium, which is linked to preventing cancer and heart disease. Pork, huh? It's practically a medicine.

A creamy, goulashy pork casserole that takes just 15 minutes of mad chopping to prepare. The subsequent 90 minutes of slow cooking means the crazy knife work becomes a distant memory and this dish feels as effortless as opening the oven door. It's a wintry, warming supper as popular with kids as with adults, but you may not want to share…

Serve with crusty bread or, if you're going to break all the rules by using two pots, it's good with spaghetti, or mashed potatoes, and a green salad.

1. Preheat the oven to 180°C/160°C fan/gas mark 4.

2. You need to find a casserole dish that you can use on the hob as well as in the oven, so probably a cast-iron one. Put it over a medium heat.

3. Heat a splash or two of olive oil in the casserole dish and throw in the pork steaks. Brown them on each side, then remove them to a plate. Add a splash more oil to the casserole dish and, when it's heated, start frying the onion, bacon and carrot, cooking them until the onion is just starting to colour.

4. Add the mushrooms and apple and cook for another minute, then return the pork steaks to the dish. Slowly pour in the cider, if using, or 200ml of the stock, if not, 'deglazing' (or scraping) the base of the casserole dish with a wooden spoon, so the lovely crusty bits sticking to the bottom go back into the sauce.

5. Pour in the remaining stock and season, probably just with pepper as stock (especially if it is from cubes) can be quite salty. Add the sage, put the lid on and pop the dish in the oven for 90 minutes.

6. Remove from the oven. Stir in the crème fraîche and sprinkle with chopped or whole sage leaves, if you like (be careful; it's strong). Serve.

The 'holy trinity' stew

Serves 6 adults

Glug of olive oil
1kg lamb shoulder, cut into
    chunky cubes
1 large onion, chopped
2 garlic cloves, crushed
1 tsp ground cumin
1 tsp ground coriander
1 cinnamon stick
1 tbsp plain flour
125ml red wine
250ml beef or lamb stock
400g tin of chopped
    tomatoes
1 tbsp honey
1 tbsp tomato purée
1 bay leaf
Small butternut squash,
    peeled, deseeded and
    chopped (see page 86)
400g tin of chickpeas,
    drained and rinsed

✳ **Freezable**

♥ **The health bit**
The clever thing about
adding tins of chickpeas,
lentils and beans to stews,
casseroles and soups is that
it's a foolproof way to boost
the nutritional value, adding
protein, B vitamins and
dietary fibre. It also makes
them stretch to feed more
people... always a bonus.

This stew is in Mumsnet Towers' all-time Top Ten. It ticks all the boxes of a chart topper. Delicious? Yes. Easy? Yes. Looks harder than it is? Ye-e-s. So it is obvious why we cook this all the time. The lamb, butternut squash and chickpeas work so perfectly together that we have nicknamed this The Holy Trinity. Amen.

1. Preheat the oven to 160°C/fan 140°C/gas mark 3.

2. In a casserole dish over a medium heat, heat the oil, then brown the lamb. You may need to do this in batches; don't crowd the pan, or the meat will stew and not brown properly. Remove the meat to a plate with a slotted spoon and repeat until it has all been browned.

3. Using the same casserole dish, lightly fry the onion and garlic in the juices left over from the meat, adding more oil if needed.

4. Once the onion has softened, stir in the spices and then the flour until it is absorbed. Slowly add the wine and stock, stirring as you go, before adding the tomatoes.

5. Now you just need to wait for the mixture to boil, before stirring in the honey, tomato purée and bay leaf. (Use sugar instead of honey if you are serving this to very young children less than one year old, see page 14.) Return the lamb and add the squash. Put the lid on and place in the oven to cook for 75 minutes.

6. Pour in the chickpeas, give it all a good stir, put the lid back on and cook for another 30 minutes.

7. Fish out the cinnamon stick and serve with crusty bread.

Lumberjack stew

Serves 6 adults

5 carrots
3 baking-type potatoes
  (about 600g in total)
2 parsnips
Glug of olive oil
800g–1kg stewing beef,
  chopped into chunky
  bite-sized pieces
1 onion, chopped
2 tbsp tomato purée
1 litre hot beef or
  chicken stock
½ tsp thyme leaves
½ tsp chopped
  rosemary leaves
2 bay leaves
Pinch of cayenne pepper
Salt and pepper
Large handful of
  frozen peas

✳ **Freezable**

Although we have never met a lumberjack, we have it on good authority that this is what they eat. All day, every day. For breakfast, lunch, dinner and possibly elevenses too. This is old-fashioned stew good and proper. The sort that kept the country alive before processed meals took over our kitchens. The slow-cooked beef, carrots, potatoes and parsnips are a delicious and hearty mix.

1. Preheat the oven to 180°C/fan 160°C/gas mark 4.

2. Peel the carrots, potatoes and parsnips and chop them. They will cook more evenly if they are the same size. That is a fact. And besides it looks nicer. Set them aside.

3. Take a large casserole dish that (ideally) has a lid, pour some oil in and, when it is hot, brown the beef in it. You may need to do this in batches; don't crowd the pan, or the meat will stew and not brown properly. Remove the meat to a plate with a slotted spoon and repeat until it is all browned. In the same oil and leftover meat juices, fry the onion slowly until soft.

4. Stir in all the chopped root vegetables and return the meat. Still with us?

5. Mix the tomato purée into the hot stock until it has dissolved. Pour it over the beef and vegetables before adding the herbs and cayenne pepper. Give it a good stir. Go on! Use those lumberjack muscles. Put a lid on the top. (If you don't have one, just use foil.)

6. Cook in the oven for three to five hours, stirring every now and then. In the meantime go for a jog, clean the house (yeah, right), or have a pootle on the internet.

7. Ten minutes before serving, season to taste and add the peas.

8. Serve. Fell a tree.

Lovely Veggies

Top ten!

- **Bean burgers**
- **Homity pie**
- **Rainbow stir-fry**
- **Thai sweet potato curry**
- **Layered aubergine bake**
- **Spinach, ricotta and tomato pasta bake**
- **Stuffed peppers**
- **Courgette fritters**
- **Cheesy leeks**
- **Hands-off tomato sauce**

If you worked out what caused the most arguments in family homes over the centuries, it wouldn't be the eldest's unsuitable boyfriends, spectacular exam fails, or whose turn it is to take out the rubbish. It would be vegetables. Day in, day out. Meal in, meal out. A low-level, life-sapping moan.

Which is such a shame. We know that sometimes there is nothing better than a bowl of Savoy cabbage, lightly cooked in butter, garlic and lemon, sprinkled with black pepper. Or steamed asparagus, drizzled with olive oil. But kids just don't get it. To many of them, vegetables are the enemy.

To help us understand children's attitude to vegetables is that often-repeated statistic that children need to try something 3,751 times before they like it. (Oh. Sorry. Apparently that's twelve times. Just with the constant moaning and threats, it *feels* like 3,751 times.) That is because there's no such thing as 'don't like'. Only 'don't like yet'. As in, 'Mummy, I don't like mushrooms.' 'No darling, you just don't like them yet.' Kids are conservative little creatures and don't really warm to anything unfamiliar. So keep on serving things. A family of four shouldn't avoid mushrooms because the three-year-old doesn't like them. The three-year-old can leave them on their plate. No biggie.

The thing is, we can only act this cavalier when we are pretty confident that what we are serving tastes nice and is something we actively want to eat, too. If we serve up boiled carrots again and again, the chances are our children are going to keep on rejecting them. We can't expect carrots to compete with chips if we just serve them steamed with no dressing.

If, however, they are carrots roasted with cumin until caramelised, then served with a sprinkling of goat's cheese, it may be that your child will start to realise they are missing out.

So we have to make vegetables delicious. This chapter is all about making them sing. Traditional British meat and two veg can be cumbersome: two piles of veg plonked on as an afterthought to the meat. Instead go exotic. Go foreign. Think Rainbow stir-fry, Layered aubergine bake, anything where the vegetables are the main attraction. And, as shocking as it may sound, add salt to those vegetables. And sugar. Obviously we're talking about a sprinkling here and there, rather than the vast quantities you get in processed food.

Talking of quantities, small plates and modest servings mean your child can decide how much they want to eat and help themselves to more. Research shows that trying to control what your child eats may cause them to become overweight. Leading by example is a far more effective way to encourage healthy eating. So, get stuck in!

And last, but not least, children and adults are meant to eat five portions of fruit and veg every day. And, no, potatoes don't count. In all cases, a portion is the amount the person can hold in the palm of their hand. It's easy to get hung up about this, but remember, a home-made smoothie can contain two portions of fruit, easy. And both houmous and baked beans count as a portion. There is a god.

Bean burgers

Glug of olive oil
½ onion, chopped
2 garlic cloves, crushed
400g tin of cannellini
 beans, or any other
 beans you have in your
 cupboard, drained
 and rinsed
1 egg, lightly beaten
Handful of breadcrumbs
 (whizz up a crustless slice
 in the food processor)
½ tbsp pesto
Pinch of chilli flakes
 (optional)
Salt and pepper

❦ Vegetarian
Make sure the pesto you use
is vegetarian.

❄ Freezable
Open-freeze the formed,
uncooked burger patties in a
single layer, then transfer to
a freezer bag for storage.

♥ The health bit
One of these burgers counts
as one of your five-a-day
servings – and they're also a
useful source of iron, which
makes them an added bonus
in a vegetarian diet.

Who needs meat? These bean burgers could seduce even the
most committed carnivore. Serve them in a bap with plenty
of sliced avocado and/or beetroot, cheese and lettuce and
open your mouth really wide...

These are particularly handy for serving to teenage
vegetarians.

1. Heat the olive oil in a frying pan and fry the onion for a couple of
minutes. Add the garlic and cook for two more minutes, or until the
onion is lightly browned.

2. In a mixing bowl, mash the beans with a fork or potato masher.
Add the egg, breadcrumbs, pesto and chilli, if using, tip in the fried
onions and garlic, season well and mix thoroughly. Chill for 10 minutes
(the burger mixture that is, not you).

3. When firm, shape into four satsuma-sized balls, or two larger patties.
Heat some more oil in the frying pan over a medium heat and pop in the
burgers. Flatten each one with a spatula into a burger shape. Cook for
about five minutes on each side, or until brown and cooked through.

Homity pie

Serves 4 adults

320g packet of ready-made
shortcrust pastry

1 tbsp flavourless vegetable
oil, plus more for the tin

Plain flour, to dust,
if needed

3 red onions (about 450g
in total), halved and
thinly sliced

2 garlic cloves, finely sliced

1 tsp thyme leaves

2 large baking-type
potatoes (about 450g
in total)

25g unsalted butter

2 tbsp finely chopped
parsley leaves

1 egg, lightly beaten

3 tbsp milk

200g Cheddar or other
hard cheese, grated

100g baby spinach

☛ **You will need**
A deep, 20cm round pie dish.

❦ **Vegetarian**
Make sure you use a
vegetarian cheese.

Potatoes, cheese, onion, all encased in buttery pastry. What's not to like? (Don't mention the spinach!) Think of this pie as your Trojan horse. Start off making it simple: comforting cheesy mash encased in pastry. And then, once you've lured your troops into a sense of security, start sneaking in other ingredients: peas, sweet potato, sweetcorn. Before you know it, you've won the vegetable war and no-one's the wiser.

Pastry can shrink when cooking, which can make a mess of your pie. To try and prevent this we 'rest' it. This means putting it in the fridge so the gluten relaxes.

1. Take the pastry out of the fridge 30 minutes before you need it. Lightly oil a deep, 20cm pie dish, or use a cake tin. It will work, trust us.

2. If your pastry is in a block, roll it out on a floured surface so it's large enough to line the base and sides of the dish. If you're using ready-rolled pastry it may be a bit short along one side, so just tear off excess pastry from elsewhere and patch it on... we're going for the rustic look. In either case, leave the pastry hanging over the sides of the dish at this point.

3. Pop the whole lot in the fridge to rest for 10 minutes. Meanwhile, preheat the oven to 200°C/fan 180°C/gas mark 6.

4. Take the dish from the fridge. Roughly trim the pastry, as in the photo.

5. Heat the 1 tbsp of oil in a frying pan, and cook the onions over a medium heat for around 10 minutes, stirring occasionally, until they are soft. Add the garlic and thyme and cook for another five minutes.

6. Meanwhile, chop the potatoes into fairly small chunks, leaving the skin on for extra nutrients (OK, we're lazy). Boil in a saucepan for 15 minutes, or until tender. Drain and set aside to cool for a few minutes.

7. Lightly mash the potatoes and add the onion mixture, butter, parsley, egg, milk, and half the cheese. Stir in the baby spinach, mixing well.

8. Transfer the mixture to the pastry case and spread out into an even layer. Top with the remaining cheese and bake in the oven for 25–30 minutes, until the cheese is crisp and the pastry crust is fully cooked.

Rainbow stir-fry

For the sauce

150ml coconut milk
2 tbsp fish sauce (optional)
3½ tbsp lime juice, or to taste
1½ tbsp soy sauce, or to taste
2 tsp brown sugar, or to taste

For the stir-fry

Glug of vegetable oil
1 red onion, finely chopped
3 garlic cloves, crushed
2.5cm piece of root ginger,
   finely grated
1 carrot, finely sliced
6 mushrooms, sliced
1 small head of broccoli,
   cut into florets
1 red pepper, sliced
200g baby spinach
Handful of toasted
   cashew nuts (optional)
Handful of Thai basil
   leaves, or half basil,
   half coriander leaves

❦ Vegetarian

Leave out the fish sauce.

♥ The health bit

Stir-frying is a great way to
cook vegetables: because they
are cooked without water, it
stops B and C vitamins being
lost. The oil makes it easier
for us to absorb fat-soluble
vitamins and phytochemicals.

This dish is a hit with kids. Perhaps it's the child-friendly name. Or the slurpy noodles it is served with. It probably isn't the long list of vegetables in the ingredients, but the delicious salty-sweet sauce takes care of them. It's perfect for a wholesome midweek supper. Chocolate cake for pud.

Obviously you can add whatever vegetables you want, or have in the fridge, to this. But remember that you want everything to fry at the initial stage rather than steam, so you can't add too many extra ingredients. If you put too much into a wok or saucepan, the elements will steam wetly rather than fry crisply.

1. Pour all the sauce ingredients in a bowl and stir well, so the sugar dissolves. Give it a taste and make sure it tastes good; add more lime juice if it's too sweet or too salty, or you might want more soy sauce if you're leaving out the fish sauce for a vegetarian version.

2. Put a wok or large frying pan on the hob and add the oil. Swirl it round, then add the onion, garlic and ginger. Stir-fry for one to two minutes, then add the carrot, mushrooms and one-quarter of the sauce. Fry for another two to three minutes.

3. Add the broccoli, red pepper and half the remaining sauce and cook for another couple of minutes. Then add the spinach and a little more of the sauce. Simmer until the spinach has wilted, then taste.

4. Throw in a little more sugar if you think it's too salty, or more lime if it's too sweet. Add the cashews, if those you're serving this to are more than five years old (see page 14). Serve with egg noodles – or stir the drained noodles through the stir-fry, as in the photograph, if you prefer – and top the lot with the herbs.

Thai sweet potato curry

Serves 2 adults

1 onion, chopped
2 tbsp flavourless oil,
   such as vegetable oil
2 tbsp red Thai curry paste
3 sweet potatoes, chopped
   (about 450g in total)
400ml tin of coconut milk
200ml vegetable or
   chicken stock
200g frozen peas

❦ **Vegetarian**
Make sure your Thai curry
paste is vegetarian (many
contain fish sauce).

♥ **The health bit**
Sweet potatoes get their
distinctive reddish-orange
colour from betacarotene,
a phytochemical which can
be converted into vitamin A
in the body. Vitamin A has a
number of vital roles helping
to keep our immune system
healthy, and just one sweet
potato provides more than
50 per cent of a child's daily
needs. Sweet potatoes also
provide useful amounts of
vitamin C, potassium and
dietary fibre.

This is a great dish to teach to older children who are about to
leave home for the first time. It's cheap, tasty, full of vitamins and
will ensure they won't starve or (worse) come back home to you
every night expecting a three-course meal. For the rest of us,
it's a great midweek supper, or a bolster to pad out a cheeky
Thai takeaway.

1. In a large saucepan or sauté pan over a medium-low heat, fry the
onion in the oil until soft.

2. Add the curry paste and fry for another minute.

3. Tip in the sweet potatoes, give it a good stir, then pour in the coconut
milk and stock. Bring to the boil, then reduce the heat and simmer for
about 15 minutes, or until the potatoes are cooked through.

4. Five minutes before serving, stir in the peas.

Layered aubergine bake

Serves 4 adults

3 baking-type potatoes
  (about 600g in total),
  chopped into chunks
1 aubergine, in slices as
  thick as a pound coin
Glugs of olive oil
500g spinach
Juice of ½ lemon
200g feta cheese
Pepper
1 tsp thyme leaves
2 garlic cloves, sliced
Handful of parsley leaves,
  roughly chopped
100ml single cream
20g hard cheese, such as
  Parmesan or Cheddar,
  finely grated

♥ **Vegetarian**

Make sure all the cheeses
you use are vegetarian.

♥ **The health bit**

Despite what Popeye would
have us believe, spinach isn't
all that good a source of iron.
On the upside it is packed
with lots of other good stuff,
including B vitamins, vitamin
C, vitamin K (important for
bone health), cancer-fighting
phytochemicals and the
minerals magnesium and
zinc. Phew!

This dish involves a lot of chopping, significant amounts of prep and lots and lots of saucepans. But on the upside, it's delicious! And your children will eat large quantities of spinach without complaining. They may even ask for seconds. And they won't even question the aubergines. Suddenly, all that effort seems worth it.

1. Heat a pan of water and, once it simmers, add the potatoes. Return to the boil and boil for 15 minutes. Drain in a colander and run cold water over them. Once they are cool, slice them as thick as a pound coin.

2. In a frying pan, fry the aubergine slices on both sides in as little olive oil as possible until they brown, then set aside.

3. Pop the spinach in a big pan that has a lid with the lemon juice, cover and put it over a medium-high heat. Let it wilt; set aside.

4. Preheat the oven to 180°C/fan 160°C/gas mark 4.

5. Using a fork, break up the feta in a small bowl. Season with pepper and add the thyme.

6. Find an ovenproof dish: if it is a lasagne-style dish, you'll probably get one layer of each ingredient; if it's a round casserole dish, you may manage two. Start with the potatoes. Then sprinkle over most of the feta, add a layer of spinach, then a neat layer of aubergines, sprinkled with the remaining feta. At regular intervals, sprinkle in some garlic, parsley or a glug of cream. Make sure none of the garlic is right on top, or it will burn.

7. Bake in the oven for about 20 minutes, then scatter the Parmesan or Cheddar over the top and bake for another 15 minutes. Serve with a salad and watch your five-a-day-ometer go through the roof.

Spinach, ricotta and tomato pasta bake

Serves 4 adults

1 onion, chopped
Glugs of olive oil
2 x 400g tins of
   chopped tomatoes
1 tsp caster sugar
Salt and pepper
150g frozen spinach,
   thawed and chopped
150g ricotta cheese
200g pasta shapes
   (any work well...
   maybe not spaghetti)
100g mozzarella
   cheese, grated
Handful of grated
   Parmesan or other
   hard cheese
Handful of breadcrumbs

✔ Vegetarian
Make sure all the cheeses
you use are vegetarian.

The razzmatazz in this pasta bake comes from the ricotta cheese, but this recipe is not prescriptive, so feel free to add and subtract as you please. It may be straight out of the 1990s, but we like to eat this with a rocket and Parmesan salad, and garlic bread.

1. Preheat the oven to 180°C/fan 160°C/gas mark 4.

2. Fry the onion in some olive oil in a large saucepan over a medium heat, until soft. Add the tomatoes, sugar, another glug of olive oil, salt and pepper and let it simmer until reduced and rich (about 20 minutes).

3. Add the spinach and cook for five more minutes, then spoon in the ricotta, stirring until it has added its gorgeous creaminess.

4. Meanwhile, boil the pasta in salted water, according to the packet instructions. Mix the mozzarella, Parmesan and crumbs in a small dish.

5. Drain the pasta and stir it into the tomato sauce, making sure everything is evenly coated. Pour into an ovenproof dish.

6. Sprinkle the mozzarella mixture evenly over the top and bake in the oven for 15–20 minutes, or until golden and bubbling. Of course this dish can be assembled in advance, covered and kept in the fridge until you need it, but you will need to up the cooking time accordingly to about 30–40 minutes. In either case, let it stand for five minutes before serving

Stuffed peppers

Serves 4 adults

4 red peppers
2 x 400g tins of haricot
   beans, drained and rinsed
200g mozzarella or
   gorgonzola cheese
Handful of torn basil leaves
Salt and pepper

Vegetarian
Make sure all the cheeses
you use are vegetarian.

The health bit
Red peppers are a veritable
superhero of the vegetable
world. Each one has twice as
much vitamin C as an orange:
just one pepper provides
more than 100 cent of your
daily needs. If you're tossing
up between which cheese to
use, mozzarella is better
for kids than gorgonzola
on the salt front.

Back in the 1980s, vegetarians had two choices when dining out:
stuffed peppers or stuffed peppers. Quite understandably this
has made them a culinary no-go area for many, which is a shame
because a well-stuffed pepper is a beautiful thing. Especially when
filled with beans.

   If you're on a budget, just buy value baked beans instead of
cannellini beans and rinse them thoroughly to get rid of the
tomatoey gloop; no one will ever know!

1. Preheat the oven to 180°C/fan 160°C/gas mark 4.

2. Slice the tops off the peppers and set the tops aside. With a small sharp
knife, remove the cores, pithy whitish ribs and seeds from their insides.
If you also need to slice a teeny bit off the bottom so they stand upright
in the baking dish, do so, but don't make a hole or they will leak.

3. Tip the beans into a mixing bowl and mash them with a fork. Tear
or crumble in the cheese and mix in the basil. Grind in some pepper
and taste the mixture: if you're using gorgonzola, you probably won't
need any extra salt, but you might if you're using mozzarella.

4. Use the mixture to stuff the peppers. Stand them in an ovenproof
dish in which they will fit snugly. Place the 'lids' back on top and cover
the dish loosely with foil. Bake for one hour.

5. Remove the foil and bake for a further 15 minutes, until the peppers
are lightly charred and deliciously sweet. Serve with a green salad.

Courgette fritters

Serves 4 adults

2 large courgettes (375g
  total weight), grated
Salt and pepper
Finely grated zest of
  2 unwaxed lemons
4 spring onions, thinly sliced
2 garlic cloves, crushed
50g Cheddar cheese, grated
Leaves from a small bunch
  of mint, chopped
2 eggs, lightly beaten
140g plain flour
Vegetable oil, to shallow-fry
Houmous or sweet chilli
  sauce, to serve

♥ Vegetarian

Make sure all the cheeses
you use are vegetarian.

♥ The health bit

Courgettes are often
well received by children
(particularly when mashed
with feta cheese). The reason
is that they taste quite mild.
Lots of other greens, such as
broccoli and cauliflower, can
be too bitter for them. But
don't worry, this aversion to
bitterness disappears as they
grow up. One day they'll be
tucking into steamed curly
kale. Probably...

If you've got a courgette, an egg and some plain flour, then you've got courgette fritters, which are both easy to make and really accommodating. You can add just about anything you've got in the fridge: feta, parsley, lime, just bung them in. And out of the frying pan comes something delicious and healthy.

1. Put the courgettes into a bowl and add a pinch of salt, the lemon zest, spring onions, garlic, cheese and mint, then mix in the eggs.

2. Gradually add the flour, mixing all the time: you may not use it all, you need just enough to give a thick batter. (If you have large courgettes, or they are a bit spongy in the middle and you can see the seeds, they might have a high water content; this means you might need more flour to get a batter consistency. If your courgettes are small and fresh they may need a little less.) Your batter will never be particularly firm, but you don't want it to be too sloppy. Season with pepper.

3. Heat the oil in a large frying pan over a medium heat and drop the courgette mixture in, a large spoonful at a time, to make 10–12 fritters. Unless your frying pan is pretty huge, you will have to do this in batches. Small fritters are less daunting for little children and are also good for dipping; large fritters are great for a heartier meal. Fry until the underside is golden brown, then turn and repeat on the other side. It takes about two minutes on each side, but you may have to increase or reduce the heat, especially for subsequent batches, to get an even colour without scorching. Remove to a plate lined with kitchen paper, to blot excess oil, then keep the cooked fritters warm in a single layer on a plate in an oven preheated to 150°C/fan 130°C/gas mark 2 while you cook the rest.

4. Serve with houmous or sweet chilli sauce.

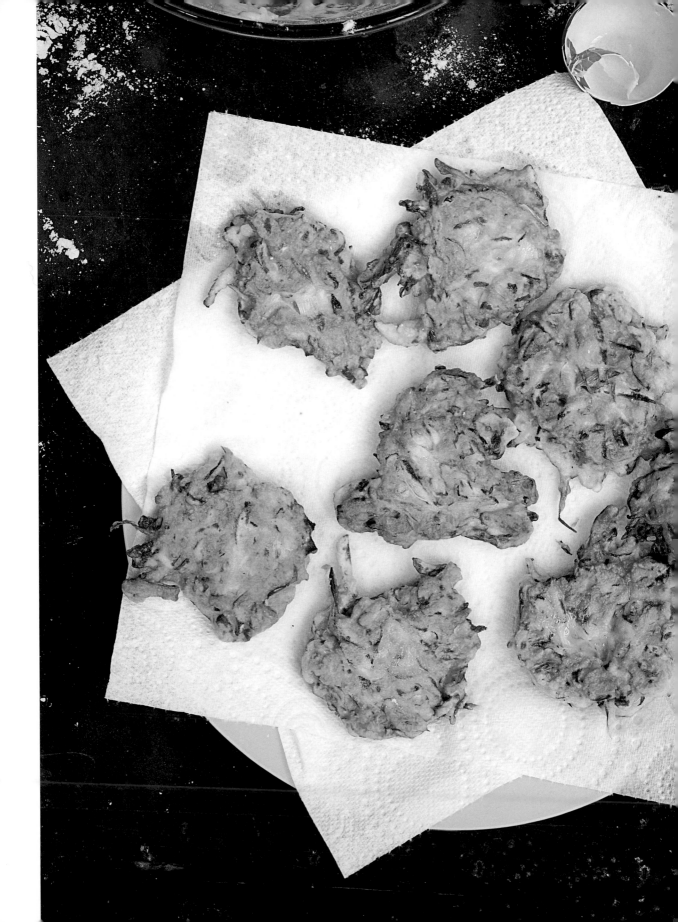

Cheesy leeks

Serves 4 adults
as a side dish

2 regular leeks or 110g
  packet of baby leeks
100ml vegetable
  or chicken stock
1 tbsp cream cheese (plain
  or with garlic and herbs)
Salt and pepper

♥ **Vegetarian**
Use vegetable stock.

♥ **The health bit**
Leeks are full of vitamin C
(immunity), B6 (hair, eyes,
skin and liver) and folic acid
(recommended for women
trying for a baby and in the
early stages of pregnancy).

Leeks are the national vegetable of Wales. And seeing how delicious they are, given the right treatment, it's no surprise that the Welsh have claimed them as their own. Here, they are lightly poached in stock before simply having cream cheese stirred through them.

1. Trim the leeks. If you are using normal leeks, slice them either lengthways or horizontally into rounds; baby leeks can be left whole.

2. In a small saucepan, cook the leeks in the stock until they are tender. Strain through a colander, reserving the cooking liquid. Keeping the leeks in the colander for a moment, put the cream cheese into the pan, adding enough of the reserved cooking liquid to make a consistency you like, then season to taste. Return the leeks and stir through. This is delicious as a side dish or – if you want to add meat to the mix – poured over cooked chicken pieces or pork chops.

Hands-off tomato sauce

Makes enough for 8 adult portions of pasta

2 x 400g tins of
  chopped tomatoes
400g tin of haricot beans,
  drained and rinsed
300ml vegetable stock
2 celery sticks, chopped
2 carrots, chopped
2 garlic cloves, chopped
Large sprig of rosemary
1 tsp brown sugar
Splash of Worcestershire
  sauce or balsamic vinegar

❦ Vegetarian

❉ **Freezable**
Freeze in smallish portions,
so it can be whipped out and
used for a last-minute pasta.

♥ **The health bit**
Think of this sauce as an
invisible cloak; all manner
of good things are hidden
beneath it. Tinned tomatoes
are rich in the phytochemical
lycopene, believed to have
cancer-fighting properties;
they are also a source of
vitamin B6, needed to
convert food into energy
and for the manufacture
of red blood cells.

This sauce is made in the oven, hence the title. It wants to be alone: no prodding or stirring, just baking. Pop all the ingredients in the pot, bung in the oven. Do something else. Then stick the sauce on pasta or pizza and watch it disappear. The Worcestershire sauce or balsamic vinegar gives it a lip-smacking savoury depth.

1. Preheat the oven to 200°C/fan 180°C/gas mark 6.

2. Put all the ingredients, except the Worcestershire sauce or balsamic vinegar, in a casserole dish that has a lid. Pop the lid on. Bake in the oven for 90 minutes. Go on then, give it a stir, but just once or twice in the whole cooking time.

3. Take it out of oven and remove the rosemary sprig. Whizz with a hand-held blender until smooth and stir in splashes of Worcestershire sauce or balsamic vinegar, to taste. Serve on pasta or home-made pizza (see page 216).

Slow
Cooking

Top ten!

- **Cowgirl stew**
- **Beef stifado**
- **Keep-it-simple kleftiko**
- **Luscious lamb shanks**
- **12-hour pulled pork**
- **Really garlicky chicken**
- **Totally inauthentic Mexican chicken**
- **Virtuous chilli**
- **No-stirring risotto**
- **Spanish potatoes**

There are few culinary questions more divisive than 'Should I buy a slow cooker?' Answers range from 'They are the saving grace of working mothers everywhere,' to 'What is this… slurry?' And it's true that, whatever colour the ingredients were when they went in the slow cooker, everything does have a tendency to come out rather brown. But brown is good! Brown is delicious! And if brown really bothers you, throw some frozen peas or green beans in near the end of the cooking time, so they don't lose their colour.

The slow cooker dream is that you bung some ingredients in the pot before work or school and then, at the end of the day, you have a delicious, nutritious meal. And most of the time that is the case. Cheap cuts of beef and lamb can take as much slow cooking as you can throw at them: the slow, gentle heat transforms them into tasty, tender stews and casseroles. But more delicate types of meat, such as chicken, can't. Don't pop them in the cooker for hours and expect them to withstand the onslaught. Stick to recommended cooking times and, if that is less than a working day, then make those recipes at the weekend and stick to dishes with a longer cooking time during the week.

What slow cookers are brilliant at is the 'their tea = your supper' conundrum. Fed up with cooking two separate meals, one for them and one for you? A slow cooker is the answer. Assemble a big casserole in the morning (or the night before and put it in the fridge) and pop it in the slow cooker before leaving home. Drum roll, please… By their tea time the house will be filled with delicious smells and the kids can be fed with virtually no effort. Then throw in a few more herbs, some Tabasco or chilli powder, and your dinner is ready a few hours later.

Buying a slow cooker won't break the bank, so even if you cook just one casserole or stew a week, it's probably worth the investment. They come in a range of sizes but a good family size is about 3.5 litres. Although if you're going to get annoyingly efficient and start batch cooking and freezing, then you could get one of the gigantic 6.5-litre behemoths.

If you're using a slow cooker for the first time, it's important to remember that there is an art to it. It's a different method of cooking: slow gentle heat in a sealed environment works differently to the hot, dry heat of a conventional oven. If you are adding large quantities of stock or wine, make sure it's hot before you put it in, as the gentle temperature of the slow cooker may not heat it up quickly enough. And don't keep opening the pot to give it a prod, because every time you lift the lid you break the seal and have to add an extra 20 minutes to the cooking time.

Other top tips include: don't add too much liquid, especially if you're converting a favourite oven recipe for the slow cooker. Liquid doesn't ever evaporate from slow cookers, so once it's in there, it's not going to disappear. And remember that, strangely, root vegetables can take longer to cook than even the cheapest cuts of meat. So don't leave them too big, chop them up into uniform sizes and put them at the base of the cooker, under the meat and nearer the heat element, so that they get more of a blast. Many casserole recipes recommend that you brown the meat in a frying pan before putting it into the slow cooker. We can reveal that the sky won't fall in if you skip this stage and that you'll have less washing up to do as well as more time to yourself – well, for other non-cooking chores, anyway – in the morning.

Cowgirl stew

Serves 4 adults

3 large carrots, sliced

1 onion, chopped

6 good-quality sausages,
   each cut into 3

2 Polish kabanos, or
   2 small chorizos, sliced

Handful of red lentils,
   green lentils or
   pearl barley

400g tin of baked beans

2 x 400g tins of
   chopped tomatoes

Couple of glugs of
   Worcestershire sauce

2 garlic cloves, sliced

Salt and pepper

400ml lager or vegetable
   or chicken stock, heated

✳ **Freezable**

♥ **The health bit**

This baby counts as three
of your recommended five
portions of fruit and veg a
day. Serve it with some green
beans for added colour and
crunch and you've hit the
heady heights of four portions.

This stew (why should cowboys get all the fun?) is a winner, and
dead easy to throw together. It takes eight hours to slow cook on
low so, if you are the organised type, you can make it before work
or the school run and it will be ready in time for tea. There is no
need to do any side dishes because it is full of fibre and has both
beans and lentils in it. That means less washing up.

1. Arrange the carrots on the bottom of the slow cooker. Arrange the
onion, sausages and kabanos or chorizos over them, then sprinkle the
lentils or barley on top. Spoon out the baked beans in a layer, then do
the same for the tinned tomatoes. Add the Worcestershire sauce and
garlic and season fairly generously to taste.

2. Pour over the heated lager or stock (if the food is still not fully covered,
top up with some water).

3. Put the lid on the slow cooker, set it to low and leave to cook all day,
or for at least eight hours.

Beef stifado

Serves 4 adults

2 tbsp plain flour
Salt and pepper
500g braising steak,
  cut into cubes
2 tbsp olive oil
10 shallots, quartered
Slug of red wine
1 tbsp red wine vinegar
1 tsp ground cinnamon
1 tsp ground allspice
3 garlic cloves, crushed
2 bay leaves
2 tbsp tomato purée

❄ **Freezable**

♥ **The health bit**

Using wine to cook for kids, are we crazy? Fear not. Most of the alcohol cooks off. There's a chance a minuscule amount will remain. If you are still worried, replace the wine with balsamic vinegar. (Boozy desserts, such as a sherry trifle, are a different matter. The alcohol isn't cooked so won't disappear.) On another note, red meat gets a bad rap, but the statistics are that one in four women have a low iron store. Although you can get iron from green veg, it is harder for your body to absorb than the stuff in red meat. So tuck in!

You may have children, but you still have a social life. Well, kind of. Socialising is tricky when you're on your knees with exhaustion by 8pm. But this flavoursome Greek beef stew could be the answer. Quick and easy, all you have to do is pop the ingredients in the slow cooker in the morning and forget about it until that night. Finding some friends who aren't too knackered to come to dinner is the hardest part.

1. Season the flour with salt and pepper, place on a shallow dish and use it to coat the chunks of beef, shaking them to remove excess.

2. Pour the oil into a large frying pan over a medium heat. Once it's heated up, add the meat and fry until brown. Do this in batches if necessary; the pan should not be crowded, or the meat will stew rather then brown properly. Remove the meat to a plate with a slotted spoon and repeat until it is all browned.

3. Place the shallots in the slow cooker and add the wine (it's hard to spoil this recipe with too much wine), the vinegar, cinnamon, allspice, garlic, bay leaves and tomato purée. Add the meat and any juices that have come from it and give everything a stir.

4. Put the lid on the slow cooker and set it to low. Cook for eight hours, but longer is fine if you're out, as this is a very forgiving dish.

5. Serve with mashed potato or, if you're feeling authentic, do what the Greeks do and serve it with pasta.

Keep-it-simple kleftiko

Serves 4 adults

1 boneless half-shoulder
  of lamb (about 800g)
500ml hot chicken stock
400g tin of chopped
  tomatoes
140g tin of tomato purée
1 large onion, chopped
4 garlic cloves, each
  cracked with the flat
  side of a knife
5 bay leaves
1 tbsp finely chopped
  rosemary leaves
1 tbsp dried oregano
Salt and pepper
Handful of parsley leaves,
  roughly chopped
200g feta cheese

✳ **Freezable**
The kleftiko can be frozen
before the feta is added.

♥ **The health bit**
It's those tinned tomatoes
again! Who knew something
found in every storecupboard
was so good for you? It's
the tinning process that
does it, breaking down the
tomatoes' cell walls so their
phytochemicals (such as
lycopene, believed to protect
against types of cancer) are
available for your body to use.

Here you are living the slow cooker dream. Bung all the ingredients in the pot in the morning – the only prep is a bit of onion chopping (or cheat and buy frozen ready-chopped onions from the supermarket) – switch the cooker on and eight hours later you and the kids have a dinner to die for. For the lamb, get the butcher to take the bone out for you, or buy it boneless from the supermarket. Allow around 200g of meat per adult.

You may be left with a lot of gravy, so have it the next day as a delicious soup. Just throw in a few handfuls of Puy lentils and simmer in a saucepan on the hob for 20 minutes.

1. Place the meat in the slow cooker and make sure it doesn't fill the cooker by more than two-thirds. Add all the other ingredients except the parsley and feta cheese.

2. Put the lid on the slow cooker and set it to low. Let the casserole cook for seven to eight hours.

3. After the casserole has cooked, check to see how oily it is. Cheap cuts of lamb can be quite fatty so, if there is a layer of oil on the top, use a spoon to scoop it away. To avoid blocked drains, place the oil in a cup or bowl and wait for it to cool and solidify before spooning it out and throwing it into the bin.

4. To serve, break up the lamb – it should be so tender you can just use a spoon – and put into bowls or plates. Strain the gravy, then spoon it over the meat. Then sprinkle with the parsley, crumble the feta on top and serve with a salad, crusty bread or new potatoes.

Luscious lamb shanks

Serves 2 adults

Glug of olive oil
2 lamb shanks
400g tin of chopped tomatoes
3–4 carrots, chopped
2 red or yellow peppers, chopped
2 onions, chopped
2 garlic cloves, crushed
Sprig of rosemary
Salt and pepper
400ml hot chicken stock

✻ **Freezable**

A few years ago – before they were rediscovered by celebrity chefs – butchers couldn't give away lamb shanks. These days they are rightly popular again, but one of the downsides of fashion is that the price has gone up. Supply and demand, eh? But they are still good value. This recipe is one of Mumsnet's favourites. The slow-cooked meat falls off the bone and the tomatoey sauce makes it a winner with the whole family.

Even after a greedy helping, there will be plenty of sauce left. Reduce it in a pan the next evening, then serve it with pasta.

1. Place a frying pan over a medium heat and add the oil. When it is hot, add the lamb shanks and cook, turning, to brown all sides.

2. Add the rest of the ingredients except the stock to the slow cooker, seasoning well, and pop the lamb shanks on top. Pour over the stock.

3. Put the lid on the slow cooker and set it to low. Cook for eight hours. Eat with mashed potato and peas.

12-hour pulled pork

Makes enough for at least 6 buns, depending on the size of the pork shoulder

2 tbsp brown sugar
1 tbsp smoked paprika
1 tsp chilli powder
1 tsp cayenne pepper
2 garlic cloves, crushed
Salt and pepper
1 boneless pork
    shoulder joint
100ml hot chicken stock,
    apple juice, cider or water

To serve
6 soft floury buns
Apple sauce

This is a cheap cut of pork, slow-cooked until it falls apart. You can pop it in the slow cooker on low (or medium, if your cooker has a medium setting) first thing in the morning. You'll arrive home to porky smells and succulent meat. It is even possible to serve the children at tea time on one day and leave the pork to cook for a further 24 hours before finishing the rest off. Sublime served in a squidgy bap with apple sauce. The only limit is the size of the pork shoulder joint you can fit in your slow cooker.

1. Mix the sugar, paprika, chilli powder, cayenne pepper and garlic together in a small bowl (easy on the chilli and cayenne if your children are young), add 1 tsp each of salt and pepper and rub it on to the pork.

2. Set the slow cooker to low and pour in the hot stock or other liquid.

3. Place the pork on top, pop on the lid and leave to cook for 12 hours. Remove from the slow cooker. Shred the meat with two forks; it will just fall apart. Spoon off and discard the fat from the top of the juices and mix them with the shredded meat. Serve the shredded pork in buns, with apple sauce, as pulled pork 'sliders'.

Really garlicky chicken

Serves 4 adults

8 chicken thighs
  and drumsticks
20 garlic cloves
1 tbsp olive oil
Salt and pepper
1 tsp hot, sweet, or smoked
  paprika, to taste
1 large onion, sliced

✳ **Freezable**

This recipe is for people who really love garlic. Or are really scared of vampires. It calls for 20 garlic cloves – that's five cloves per person – which means each bit of chicken is completely sozzled in garlic.

When you're using this many garlic cloves, you want their preparation to be super-quick. To take off their papery skins, forget cutting off their tails with a knife. Instead just give them a 'crack' by putting them under the flat side of a broad-bladed knife and pushing down with the heel of your hand. The garlic will break up a bit and the papery skin will flake off. They are ready to use.

1. To prepare the chicken thighs and drumsticks, remove as much of the skin as you can easily pull off, so the dish doesn't become too fatty.

2. Peel the garlic cloves by cracking each one under the flat side of a broad-bladed knife (see recipe introduction).

3. Put the chicken, garlic, oil, 1 tsp of salt, some pepper and the paprika in a large bowl and toss, so the flavoured oil covers all the ingredients.

4. Place the slices of onion on the base of the slow cooker and add the chicken mixture. You don't need to add any liquid. Put on the lid and cook for six hours on low, or four hours on high.

5. When you are ready to eat, remove the chicken from the pot with a slotted spoon. Spoon off and discard the fat from the top of the juices. Pop the slow-cooked garlic cloves and some of the cooking juices into some mashed potato for a delicious garlic mash and serve the chicken and remaining juices with green beans or peas.

Totally inauthentic Mexican chicken

Serves 4 adults

400g tin of chopped
   tomatoes
1 red onion, chopped
5 tsp ground cumin
1 garlic clove, crushed
Juice of ½ lime
450g boneless chicken,
   cut into bite-sized pieces
   (thighs are cheaper and
   juicier than breasts)
340g tin of sweetcorn,
   drained and rinsed
400g tin of kidney beans,
   drained and rinsed

❄ **Freezable**

♥ **The health bit**
Tinned sweetcorn and beans
are great storecupboard
ingredients, but make sure
you buy those that have been
tinned without added salt
or sugar. Rinse tinned beans
well in plenty of cold water
to help remove some of the
sugars that can cause wind.

For the true flavours of Mexico, go elsewhere. This recipe is Mexican-*style*. Despite that, it is truly delicious. Quick to prepare, the total lack of chilli or other heat means that kids love it. For the full multicultural inauthentic experience, serve in tacos with grated Cheddar and a dollop of Greek yogurt.

1. Make the salsa: put the tomatoes, onion, cumin, garlic and lime juice in a bowl and stir. Spread half the salsa in the base of the slow cooker.

2. Drop the chicken into the cooker. Add the sweetcorn and kidney beans, then spread the rest of the salsa on the top.

3. Put the lid on and cook on low for six hours.

4. Serve with rice or tacos, tortilla chips, coriander leaves, sour cream or Greek yogurt, guacamole, a spritz of lime or some grated cheese.

Virtuous chilli

Serves 4 adults

1 courgette, sliced
2 carrots, sliced
2 celery sticks, sliced
2 garlic cloves,
   finely chopped
1 onion, chopped
1 red pepper, chopped
Handful of mushrooms,
   roughly sliced
2 x 400g tins of whole
   plum tomatoes
400g tin of chickpeas,
   drained and rinsed
1 tsp dried oregano
2 bay leaves
1 tsp chilli powder
2 tsp ground cumin
Salt

To serve
Crème fraîche
Grated cheese

♥ **Vegetarian**

✳ **Freezable**

♥ **The health bit**
This dish provides three of
the recommended five-a-day.
But you want more, don't
you? More nutrition. In that
case, add tzatziki to temper
the heat and boost calcium
and protein intake. See? Easy.

This tastes so goooood. But that isn't why it's virtuous. It's virtuous because it's absolutely jam-packed with vegetables and pulses. Have an apple for pudding and you'll hit the jackpot as a human fruit and veg machine. Alternatively, a delicious but healthy main course like this is the perfect excuse for having Guaranteed-super-squidgy chocolate brownies (see page 307) for pud afterwards.

This is a chilli and it's got a bit of a kick, so young kids may not like it. Leave out the chilli powder and add some sweet chilli sauce at the end of cooking if you want to make it more palatable for them. Or stir in a big splodge of crème fraîche or sour cream when it's served, to calm down the heat.

1. This recipe demands a lot of chopping, so it's unlikely you'll prepare it in the morning before work or school. Do it the night before and/or delegate. Put the chopped and sliced vegetables in the slow cooker with the tomatoes, chickpeas, herbs, spices and ½ tsp of salt. Stir.

2. If you have prepared this the night before you need it, cover and pop the slow cooker bowl in the fridge overnight, then whip it out and place in the metal cooker in the morning.

3. Put the lid on your slow cooker. Cook it on high for four to six hours, or on low for six to eight hours.

4. Season and serve with crème fraîche and grated cheese. And some rice if you're really hungry.

No-stirring risotto

Serves 4 adults

1 tbsp unsalted butter,
  plus a large knob more
  to serve
1 tbsp olive oil
1 small onion,
  finely chopped
1 leek, finely sliced
1 large garlic clove,
  finely chopped
300g arborio rice
250g chestnut
  mushrooms, sliced
800ml hot vegetable
  or chicken stock
80g Parmesan or other
  hard cheese, grated
Salt and pepper

❦ **Vegetarian**
Use a vegetarian cheese
instead of the Parmesan.

♥ **The health bit**
You've virtually hit two of the
recommended five portions
of veg a day with this dish.
Not only that, but they are
well hidden among rice and
cheese! Children often find a
big pile of vegetables on the
side of their plate off-putting,
so this is a good way of
sneaking them in.

Risotto without the arm-ache? Impossible, we hear you cry!
Not any more. This leek and mushroom risotto gets the slow
cooker treatment. Normally with risotto you have to stir non-
stop, but here, after initially frying the ingredients, you bung
everything in the slow cooker and leave it for two hours.

Leek and mushrooms taste great, but for a change try bacon
and peas, or butternut squash and sage. Oh, and did we mention
there is no stirring?

Leftover risotto is delicious rolled into little balls, dusted with
flour or coated in breadcrumbs and shallow-fried in olive oil until
crisp. Make sure the risotto balls are piping hot right through,
as reheated rice can be a source of food poisoning.

1. Heat the butter and olive oil in a frying pan and fry the onion, leek and
garlic for five or six minutes, or until soft. Add the rice, stirring quickly so
each grain is coated in the oil and butter. Cook the rice for two minutes
until it becomes slightly translucent.

2. Transfer the rice mixture to the slow cooker and stir in the
mushrooms and stock. Put on the lid and cook on medium for two
hours, or until the rice is cooked and the stock properly absorbed.

3. Stir in the cheese and the knob of butter, season with salt and pepper
and serve immediately.

Spanish potatoes

Serves 4 adults as a main course, or 6 as a side dish

2 tbsp olive oil
1 red onion, finely sliced
1–2 garlic cloves, chopped
1 tsp smoked paprika
½ tsp chilli flakes
1 red pepper, chopped
1 yellow pepper, chopped
400g tin of chopped
   tomatoes
300ml hot vegetable stock
2 sprigs of thyme
50g pitted olives, black or
   green, it's up to you
Salt and pepper
550g potatoes, cut into small
   cubes (peeling optional)
Feta cheese, to serve
   (optional)

❦ Vegetarian
Make sure the feta cheese
you use is vegetarian.

❄ Freezable

♥ The health bit
Peppers are hard to beat.
As well as truly impressive
amounts of vitamin C (just
half a red pepper packs more
than 100 per cent of a child's
daily needs), they also provide
vitamin B6, betacarotene and
folic acid.

The brilliance of the potato is often overlooked in favour of more fashionable carbs. But we love a spud (our Roast potatoes on page 178 are the best in the world). Their versatility is showcased beautifully in this melt-in-your-mouth Spanish stew. It is delicious on its own, or as a side dish to go with grilled fish or roast chicken.

1. Heat the oil in a frying pan over a medium-low heat and cook the onion until soft. Stir in the garlic, paprika, chilli flakes and peppers and cook for two minutes. Add the tomatoes, stock, thyme, olives, salt and pepper and bring to the boil.

2. Put the potatoes in the slow cooker and pour over the hot tomato sauce. Pop on the lid and cook on high for four to five hours; any longer and it will get mushy. Remove the thyme sprigs.

3. Hop over the Mediterranean Sea to Greece and borrow some feta cheese to slice or crumble over the top, if you want. Serve with a green salad, some crusty bread and a glass of Cava for yourself. Olé.

Sunday Lunch

Top ten!

- **Roast pork**
- **Sunday-for-Monday baked ham**
- **One-pot lentil chicken**
- **Spinach and mushroom filo pie**
- **Courgette and fennel salad**
- **Roast potatoes**
- **Honey-roast parsnips**
- **Sweet potato gratin**
- **Yorkshire towers**
- **Goodness gravy!**

You're leaning back in your chair. Cheeks a little bit flushed. You're smiling. Shafts of light come in through the enormous windows, illuminating a table full of casually arranged but beautifully prepared food.

Cut to your children. Their heads are thrown back in laughter, pearly white teeth shine. They are definitely not saying 'poo' or 'bum'. No, the five-year-old is making a comment about the provenance of the cheese. Good friends look on, basking in the warm glow, marvelling at how you do it.

Real life? You're on your knees. The lamb should have been ready an hour ago and the damn thing is still too pink. Everything else has gone a little bit soggy and, rather than think 'sod it!' and enjoy yourself, you've apologised to everyone several times. The five-year-old is definitely saying 'poo' and 'bum'.

When you have kids, dinner parties become a thing of the past. Who can afford a babysitter and a taxi? Instead we cook Sunday lunches where the kids come, too. They are (or should be) a relaxed and intimate affair. A time to catch up with friends, get to know their children and enjoy food, wine and good company.

But the nature of a Sunday lunch is that everything is done at the last minute. Roasting the meat is the easy part, it's all the side dishes that act like little landmines, detonating along your path. Gravy, anyone?

However, there is a different way. We have pooled our resources and we think we've come up with a collection of recipes that are easy to knock together and let you enjoy yourself, too.

One-pot lentil chicken has all the taste of roast chicken, minus the faff of organising any veg, as it all goes into the pot at the beginning. Plus not one vegetable is peeled in the process. (OK, rumbled. You need to peel two onions. But not if you buy frozen chopped onions.)

Sweet potato gratin is totally prepared in advance, then just whipped out of the oven at the last minute, accompanied by steam, aroma and admiring oohs and aahs. Courgette and fennel salad needs to be made a couple of hours beforehand and left to marinate in the garlic and lemon dressing. It's a deliciously fresh accompaniment to any roast. And our definitive home-made gravy recipe will hold your hand through those crucial last minutes before serving.

But a successful Sunday lunch isn't all about the food. A lot of it is about you. Are you sobbing on the kitchen floor? That's bad. Are you smiling, despite the burning smell coming from the kitchen? That's good! Well, kind of. Better that there's no burning smell, but, if there is, you should definitely smile. And don't apologise when you serve the food: 'This was so much nicer last time I made it.' We don't care! We're just going to shove it in our gobs while talking too much and ignoring our children.

People don't gather together at Sunday lunch to dissect the culinary expertise of the chef. They gather together to chat, laugh, gossip, possibly fall off their chair, and get stuck in to whatever is put in front of them. Really, all you need to serve up is a smile. But these recipes will help.

We didn't want to waste any space in this chapter with basic lamb and beef roasts; if you do want to roast one of those, however, start by preheating the oven to a temperature of 220°C/fan 200°C/gas mark 7 and bung some sliced onions and carrots and/or celery in a roasting tray with a splash of water or wine. Plonk the joint fat-side up on top, roast for 20 minutes, then reduce the oven temperature to 160°C/fan 140°C/gas mark 3 and cook for 10 minutes per 500g for rare, 15 minutes for medium, or – if you must – 20 minutes for well-done.

Roast pork

Serves 6–8 adults,
depending on appetite

Boneless leg of pork,
  about 1kg
Salt and pepper
Glug of olive oil
2 onions, sliced

To serve
Roast potatoes
  (see page 178)
Honey-roast parsnips
  (see page 180)
Goodness gravy!
  (see page 186)

Crackling. Is there a finer word? Just the thought of its salty, crisp unctuousness has us drooling over the keyboard. It is the crowning glory of this foolproof roast pork. A taste sensation. Ask your butcher to score the rind (though you can do it yourself).

1. Take the pork out of the fridge about an hour before cooking, so it can come to room temperature (this is important when cooking any meat). Preheat the oven to 220°C/fan 200°C/gas mark 7.

2. Season the flesh of the pork with salt and pepper and rub in some olive oil, avoiding the rind. If the rind isn't scored, or the score marks are a bit far apart, score it yourself with a sharp knife (a Stanley knife is good), cutting diagonal lines about 1cm apart. Pat the rind with kitchen paper to get it as dry as possible; you want your crackling to crackle! Rub some salt into the rind, especially into the score marks. Add pepper, too, if you like peppery crackling.

3. Layer the onion slices in a roasting tin. Put the pork on top – skin-side up – making sure it covers all the onions so they don't burn.

4. Roast in the hot oven for 30 minutes. Reduce the oven temperature to 180°C/fan 160°C/gas mark 4 and cook for another 40 minutes.

5. Remove the pork from the oven. Now you can choose to leave the crackling in place or to remove it with a knife. Careful, it's hot! Cover the pork meat in foil and leave it to rest on a large plate. If the crackling needs further crisping, then flatten it out and finish it under a hot grill, watching closely to make sure it doesn't burn. Skim the juices of excess fat and use them to make the gravy (see page 186).

6. Serve the pork and crackling with Roast potatoes, Honey-roast parsnips, lashings of Goodness gravy! and some wilted spinach, lightly cooked cabbage or other greens.

Sunday-for-Monday baked ham

**Serves 6 adults,
plus lots of leftovers
(or more adults and
fewer leftovers...)**

For the ham
2kg unsmoked
  gammon joint
1 onion, halved
1 celery stick,
  roughly chopped
1 carrot, roughly chopped
4–5 black peppercorns
2 bay leaves

For the glaze
Handful of whole cloves
15g mustard powder
45g soft brown sugar

✳ **Freezable**

Of course you want to cook an extravagant feast for family and friends to enjoy as the weekend comes to a close. You want great conversation, delicious food and good wine to bring everyone together for a gloriously chaotic couple of hours. But sometimes Sunday afternoons need to be about getting a jump on the week ahead. This baked ham lets you do both. Bake a big one and eat it hot on Sunday with Honey-roast parsnips (see page 180), mash and a spot of gravy. Then use it for packed lunch sarnies and pasta bakes throughout the week. It also freezes brilliantly.

Baked ham is made using gammon, which is cured pork. It is cured using brine, which means it can be salty and, in the old days, you'd soak it overnight to make it edible. Nowadays that is not necessary, but, if you're worried, change the water halfway through the boiling stage.

When buying your ham, allow 225g per person. This is an average serving, so get a joint big enough to feed you all, plus provide some (very useful) leftovers.

1. Put the ham in a large saucepan or pot that has a lid and cover with cold water. Pop the onion, celery, carrot, peppercorns and bay leaves in with it.

2. Bring the water to the boil, then reduce the heat to a simmer and cook for 20 minutes per 450g. Drain halfway through and replace with fresh boiling water, if you are worried it may be too salty.

3. Drain and let the ham cool until you can comfortably touch the meat. Meanwhile, preheat the oven to 190°C/fan 170°C /gas mark 5.

4. Using your hands, peel the rind and outside layer of fat off the joint. It should tear off fairly easily, leaving you with an even (but not too deep) layer of fat. Score this fat with a sharp knife in a criss-cross pattern, avoiding cutting the meat. Stud each point where the lines cross (within reason!) with a clove. Or stick the clove in the middle of the squares.

5. Mix the mustard powder and sugar together well so they form a powdery rub, then smother it on to the fat.

6. Put the joint on a baking tray lined with foil (to help when washing up) and pop it in the oven for 30–40 minutes, basting it regularly.

7. Remove the ham from the oven when it's golden; don't let it burn. Keep it warm and let it rest for 15–30 minutes before carving.

One-pot lentil chicken

**Serves 4 adults,
plus leftovers**

Salt and pepper
1 chicken, about 2kg
Glug of olive oil
3 rashers of smoked
  bacon, chopped
2 onions, chopped
2 garlic cloves, chopped
1 celery heart, chopped
100g green lentils
Leaves from 1 bunch of
  parsley, chopped
400g can cannellini beans,
  drained and rinsed

❄ **Freezable**

♥ **The health bit**

Ah, lentils. So much tastier
than their reputation allows.
And, of course, they're really
good for us. In addition to
protein, they contain
B vitamins, and are a good
source of soluble fibre that
helps to reduce cholesterol.

Make it once and this dish will become a firm family favourite, we promise. Warming, savoury and easy to prepare, there's not much more you could ask of a chicken. Ten minutes prep and a couple of minutes at the end are all it takes to have a beautifully cooked pot roast, plus a bundle of deliciously flavoured accoutrements. Stir in some baby spinach at the end, if greenery is really an issue. No side dishes required.

1. Preheat the oven to 180°C/fan 160°C/gas mark 4.

2. Rub salt and pepper into the skin of the chicken. Heat a large (preferably cast-iron) casserole dish on the hob and add a little olive oil, then fry the chicken on all sides until it is slightly golden all over. Remove the chicken from the dish and put it on a plate.

3. Add the bacon, onions, garlic and celery to the casserole dish. Stir and fry over a low heat until they start to take on a little colour.

4. Remove the casserole dish from the flame, then add the lentils and half the parsley. Place the browned chicken on top of everything and pour in enough hot water from the kettle to cover the lot. Season with plenty of pepper, cover and cook in the oven for about 90 minutes.

5. When the time is up, take the dish out of the oven. Check the chicken is properly cooked by sticking a skewer in the thickest part of the thigh – the juices should run clear with no trace of pink. (If you don't think it's ready, give it another five to 10 minutes in the oven, then check again.) Tip the chicken up, using tongs, to allow any juices from the cavity to drain back into the broth (be careful they don't spill down your arm; they're hot!). Carefully remove the chicken to a dish, using both hands, with the tongs, a serving spoon or carving fork. Cover with foil and set aside to rest.

6. Heat the lentil broth on the hob and add the beans. Check the seasoning and add more if needed (pulses can take a lot of seasoning). Shred or slice the chicken, as you prefer.

7. Ladle some of the lentil broth into a wide soup dish or a bowl, arrange some sliced or shredded chicken on top and scatter with the remaining parsley. Serve and graciously accept the compliments.

Spinach and mushroom filo pie

Serves 6 adults

1 onion, chopped
2 garlic cloves, crushed
1 tbsp olive oil
500g frozen chopped
  spinach, half thawed
250g mushrooms
  (a selection of types
  is nice), sliced
Salt and pepper
100g feta or goat's
  cheese, crumbled
Leaves from 2 sprigs
  of thyme
1 tbsp unsalted butter
4 large sheets of filo pastry
  (there are normally 6
  in a packet; freeze the
  other 2)

☛ **You will need**
20cm-ish wide, non-stick
springform cake tin.

❦ **Vegetarian**
Check the cheese you use
is vegetarian.

This pie is a great veggie showstopper. If you've never cooked with filo pastry, this could be your culinary find of the year. (It's also lower in fat than shortcrust or puff.) Obviously the pastry is shop-bought. We aren't completely crazy.

1. Preheat the oven to 200°C/fan 180°C/gas mark 6.

2. Place a large frying pan over a medium heat and fry the onion and garlic in the oil until soft.

3. Add the spinach, mushrooms and salt and pepper, then fry for five more minutes.

4. Remove from the heat and let the mixture cool slightly, then add the cheese and thyme.

5. Melt the butter gently and use some of it to brush a 20cm (give or take... use what you have, don't buy a new one!) non-stick springform cake tin. Put in a sheet of filo pastry, leaving the excess hanging over the edge, then butter it. Add the remaining sheets, each at an angle to the one before, and buttering each as you go.

6. Pour in the spinach and mushroom mixture and fold the pastry over the top. A few scrunched edges of pastry are good, as they turn wonderfully crunchy in the oven. Butter the top.

7. Bake for 20–30 minutes or until golden brown. Wait five minutes before gently releasing the pie from the tin and cutting it into wedges. This is delicious served with Sweet potato gratin (see page 183).

Courgette and fennel salad

**Serves 4 adults
as a side dish**

2–3 small courgettes
1 fennel bulb
1 garlic clove, crushed
Juice of 1 lemon
Glug of extra virgin
  olive oil
1 tsp dried oregano
Salt and pepper

 Vegetarian

Shaved into long ribbons, this is courgette's 'Oh, Miss Jones!' moment. Y'know, where the previously plain-but-likeable secretary takes off her glasses, lets down her hair and suddenly everyone realises she's gorgeous? This recipe is where courgette says 'no!' to ratatouille and a husky, seductive 'yes' to fennel. Ahem, anyway. As well as being sexy, this salad goes brilliantly with a roast and *must* be made in advance, to let the flavours infuse. You know what that means? No last-minute cooking of peas and carrots!

1. Trim off the top and bottom of each courgette. Using a potato peeler, shave the courgettes lengthways into ribbons. The green skin looks lovely against the pale yellow of the flesh. If it's a big or slightly old courgette it might be a bit seedy and puffy in the middle; don't bother shaving this bit, just chuck it into the compost. Pop the ribbons into a bowl.

2. Slice off the root and the dried-out tips of the fennel bulb, reserving any frondy leaves. With a sharp knife, or a mandolin, thinly slice the fennel bulb and add to the bowl.

3. Add the garlic and mix the salad with the lemon juice, olive oil and oregano. Season. This salad benefits from generous seasoning (though perhaps not when serving children). Add any fennel fronds you reserved.

4. Ideally leave to marinate for a couple of hours, while you relax, or indeed marinate yourself in a glass of wine.

Roast potatoes

**Serves 4 adults
as a side dish**

50g goose fat, lard, fat
  from the meat you are
  roasting, or olive oil
800g floury potatoes,
  such as King Edward
Salt
1 tbsp plain flour or
  polenta (optional)

❦ Vegetarian
Use olive oil to roast
the potatoes.

We love a roastie at Mumsnet Towers. Especially a home-made roastie. Mass-produced roast potatoes never really cut it; even good gastropubs can't turn them out as well as we can at home. So it's our duty, as parents, to show our little ones the heaven that can be achieved by turning a spud into a crisp, crunchy golden ball of deliciousness. Because if we don't, who will? And if our kids don't even know real roast potatoes exist, how will they make them for us in our old age? Exactly. Get roasting.

1. Preheat the oven to its highest setting. Put the fat in a large, heavy-based roasting tin and place it in the oven.

2. Fill a large saucepan (one that has a lid) with water, put it on a high heat and bring to the boil.

3. While you're waiting for it to boil, peel the potatoes and cut them. The size is up to you, whatever you think of as roast potato-sized. The only rule is that they should all be a similar size, so they cook at the same rate.

4. Add some salt to the water in the pan and, once the water starts to boil, carefully slide the potatoes in so the water doesn't splash on you. Return to the boil, then simmer the potatoes for five to seven minutes. The outsides should become soft, but the centre will remain hard.

5. Drain the potatoes, put them back in the saucepan (off the heat) and cover for five minutes, until the potatoes turn white and floury-looking. Once this happens, sprinkle in the flour or polenta, if using. Flour will give them a crisper crust; polenta will render them explosively crunchy.

6. Hold the handle of the pan with one hand and the lid with the other. Shake the pan so the potatoes get bashed about, roughing them up a bit, which means they will be crisper once they are roasted.

7. Remove the roasting tin from the oven and put it on the hob over a medium heat. The fat should be incredibly hot now. Put the potatoes in the tin very carefully with a spoon, so they don't spit too much. Once they're in, baste them properly so they are all completely covered in fat.

8. Return to the top shelf of the oven, close the door and don't bother them for about 40 minutes, apart from turning them over at the roughly halfway point. Take them out of the oven – they should be perfectly golden all over – and sprinkle with salt. Thank goodness! The future of the roast potato is assured.

Honey-roast parsnips

**Serves 4 adults
as a side dish**

8 parsnips, peeled and cut
  into thumb-width wedges
2 tbsp plain flour
Salt and pepper
4 tbsp olive oil
2 tbsp runny honey

❦ Vegetarian

♥ The health bit
The benefits of adding honey
to carrots or parsnips
(basically that your children
may actually eat them)
outweighs any damage that
honey (which has pretty
much the same nutritional
value as sugar) can do.

Parsnips are for life, not just for Christmas. Loved in December and forgotten during the rest of the year, they are possibly the country's most under-appreciated root vegetable. Roasting them with honey creates a sweet, crunchy, chewy loveliness that will rival roast tatties in the 'seconds, please!' popularity stakes.

1. Preheat the oven to 220°C/fan 200°C/gas mark 7.

2. Bring a large pan of water to a boil, then add the parsnips and boil for five minutes. Drain well, then let them dry in a colander.

3. Mix the flour with some salt and pepper. Toss the parsnips in the flour mixture until they are nicely coated.

4. Heat the oil in a large roasting tray in the oven for five minutes. Carefully place the parsnips in the sizzling oil, turning them so they are thoroughly coated. Don't crowd them or they won't crisp up. Roast in the hot oven for 25 minutes, or until crisp, turning once.

5. Drizzle the honey over the parsnips (unless you are serving babies less than one year old, who shouldn't eat honey, see page 14), give them a little shake, then cook for a further five minutes until golden brown.

Sweet potato gratin

**Serves 6 adults
as a side dish**

1 garlic clove, halved
4–5 sweet potatoes
Glug of olive oil
Couple of handfuls of sage
  leaves, chopped
Salt and pepper
Unsalted butter, for
  greasing the dish
250ml double cream (or
  more if you're using very
  large potatoes, and less if
  you're using small ones)

 Vegetarian

Something magical happens to sweet potatoes when they are baked with cream and sage. This is a great side dish when you are entertaining, because everything's done in advance, leaving you more time to be the hostess with the mostest.

If you want to cut through some of that gooey sweetness (though the sage will help), add already-wilted, well-drained greens to the gratin before baking. Chard works well.

1. Preheat the oven to 180°C/fan 160°C/gas mark 4. Take the garlic clove and rub it around the base and sides of a shallow ovenproof gratin dish (about 15cm square is perfect). This gives lovely garlicky flavour without being too overwhelming.

2. Slice the potatoes into 1cm slices. Toss in a bowl with a splash of oil and the sage and season with salt and pepper.

3. Butter the gratin dish, then add the potato slices, overlapping them neatly on the top layer.

4. Cover with foil and bake in the oven for 30 minutes. Now remove the foil and pour the cream over so that the sweet potato is just covered. Bake for a further 30 minutes until golden on top, checking regularly so that it does not scorch or dry out. Season with pepper if you like, then leave the gratin to rest and firm up a little for 15 minutes before serving.

Yorkshire towers

Makes 10–12

Flavourless oil, such as
  vegetable oil
2 eggs
Salt and pepper
About 250ml milk
100g plain flour, sifted

☛ **You will need**

A Yorkshire pudding tray.

❦ **Vegetarian**

❄ **Freezable**

Cool the Yorkshire towers
completely after cooking.
Open-freeze in a single layer,
then transfer to a freezer
bag for storage. Reheat in
the Yorkshire pudding tray
in an oven preheated to
180°C/fan 160°C/gas mark 4
until hot right through.

To call these Yorkshire puddings would be a huge understatement.
Instead they are Yorkshire towers. Batter skyscrapers. And the
best you'll taste outside God's Own County. You'll never buy
frozen again.

The batter can be covered and stored in the fridge until needed;
don't worry if it greys or separates, you can just whisk it again
before you use it.

1. Preheat the oven to its highest setting. Put a little vegetable oil into
each hole of a Yorkshire pudding tray and put in the hot, hot, hot oven
until the oil is smoking. This is important.

2. Crack the eggs into a large measuring jug and add the salt and pepper.
Top the mixture up with milk until it reaches the 300ml mark.

3. Add the flour gradually, whisking all the time so you don't get lumps.
You can use a hand-held or electric whisk if that's easier.

4. Carefully (using oven gloves) pour the batter into each hole of the
smoking hot Yorkshire pudding tray until it is about halfway full.
Then – no dilly-dallying – whack them straight back into the oven.
Monitor their progress, but don't open the door. They are ready when
golden brown and puffed up, after 20–30 minutes.

Goodness gravy!

**Serves 4–6 adults
as an accompaniment**

The juices and root
  vegetables from
  under a roast
3 tsp plain flour
Small glass of wine, cider
  or port, depending on
  the meat (see right)
1 litre hot stock

Optional extras
Mustard
Anchovies
Redcurrant jelly

✱ **Freezable**

Have your guests arrived already? Are they sitting there, expectantly, while you read this? If so, never fear, gravy is easy. Get out the packet of gravy granules, add hot water and the meat juices from the roasting tin. Et voila! You've done it. Now off you hop and enjoy yourself.

If you're still reading and have a little more time on your hands, there is an alternative. It is marginally more complicated and needs a little bit of forethought, but it's worth it.

To make the gravy as delicious as possible, make it complement the meat. For pork, use cider or perhaps add an apple or two to the vegetables under the joint of meat. Red wine is the obvious choice of alcohol for beef and a spoon of horseradish or mustard stirred in at the end would work well, too. Lamb is another candidate for red wine, and maybe an anchovy stirred in at the end for an umami hit. Chicken can pretty much take whatever you throw at it, but white wine is the classic, with Dijon mustard.

Things to do in advance

1. When roasting your meat (such as Roast pork, see page 169), cook it on a bed of vegetables. Onion, carrot and celery are good. These will be used later in your gravy.

2. Measure out your gravy ingredients in advance and have the water for the stock boiling in the kettle. That way making gravy is just throwing some ingredients into a pan, rather than a last-minute panic which involves willing a kettle to boil, trying to find a clean jug to make the stock in, then realising you've run out of stock cubes.

To make the gravy

3. Take the meat out of the roasting tin and cover it loosely with foil, so that it rests and keeps warm.

4. Remove as much fat from the roasting tin as possible (the fat is the clear liquid which floats to the surface). The no-washing-up way is to tip the tin away from you and use a soup spoon to ladle up the fat. The fusspot's way is to decant the juices into a jug, wait for the fat to come to the top, then blot it off with layers of kitchen paper before returning the defatted juices to the roasting tin. You decide.

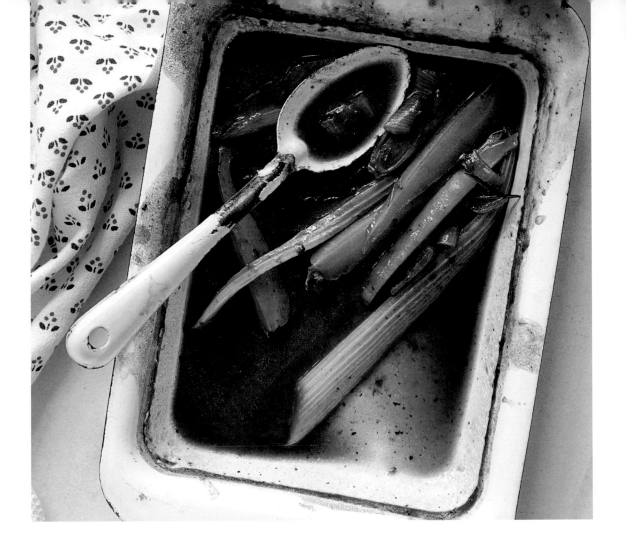

5. Place the tin with its vegetables and the meat juices over a medium heat on the hob and stir in the flour. Using the tines of a fork, mash up the vegetables as much as you can. It won't look much like gravy at the moment. Now add the glass of alcohol and allow the mixture to come to a simmer for a minute, so the booze burns off.

6. Add the stock to the gravy and return it to the boil. Keep scraping the bottom of the roasting tin with a wooden spoon to incorporate all the crunchy bits of flavour. Reduce the heat and simmer for 10 minutes. By now it should be looking more like gravy.

7. Strain the liquid through a sieve into a saucepan, using the wooden spoon to press as much of the vegetable goodness through as possible.

8. There's your gravy. Heat it up when you are ready to serve and add a dollop of mustard/an anchovy/some redcurrant jelly, depending on what you fancy and which meat you're serving.

Fast Food

Top ten!

- **Spaghetti with pesto, peas and pancetta**
- **Life-saving noodles**
- **Curried baked beans**
- **Lazy days couscous**
- **Garlic mushrooms**
- **Italian baked chicken**
- **Origami fish**
- **Mackerel pâté**
- **Simple soda bread**
- **60-second cheesecake**

N o, not *that* sort of fast food. This is real, proper, healthy food that doesn't tax your time, brain or culinary skills. Supermarkets, retailers and companies with scarily massive marketing budgets would have you believe our ancestors haven't been feeding themselves perfectly well (and without their help) for the last few millennia…

Cooking for you and your family needn't be akin to the thirteenth labour of Hercules. With clever shopping, a bit of list making, some good recipes and a modicum of organisation, you can cook a meal for four in the time it takes to walk to the corner shop for some waffles and frozen pancakes.

We thought long and hard about this chapter. Quick and easy recipes are certainly the most popular both on our own blog and on the Mumsnet food pages. So we realise it is all about balancing speed with results. That is why most of these dishes take less than 10 minutes to prepare. They may take longer to cook, but in terms of chopping, stirring and pouring, there is a 10-minute watershed.

It can seem a slog to get dinner on the table every evening (not to mention breakfasts and lunches too), but it needn't take long and – dare we say it? – it can even be fun.

So, what you need to remember is:

- Shop cleverly. As you wheel your trolley around the supermarket, think in terms of meals, not random items that you quite like the look of. It is frighteningly easy to pootle around, spend £100, get home and realise you have *nothing* for dinner that night… but that you have shopping bags bulging with a bottle of lemon cordial, basmati rice and four boxes of dishwasher tablets that were on offer.

- Go with a few recipes in mind and having made a list of their essential components. We like taking photos of ingredients lists on our phones, so we can spot-check what we need. It is also a good idea to have some staples in the cupboard to fall back on. In our fridge, freezer and pantry (OK, it is just a cupboard) we always have: couscous for Lazy days couscous; frozen prawns and straight-to-wok noodles for Life-saving noodles; and pesto and frozen peas for Spaghetti with pesto, peas and pancetta. Oh, and tins of sweetcorn.

- Then there are those shortcut 'cheat' ingredients that make complicated dishes easier. Such as frozen chopped onions or tins of ready-cooked onions (yes, really), garlic-infused oil and shop-bought pastry.

- We know that sometimes you need something sweet and fast. So we have included our favourite instant cheesecake. Genius, huh?

- Food doesn't have to be about cooking, it can be about simply assembling. A plate of sliced tomatoes, some ham and crusty bread can be more satisfying than a dish that took far longer to prepare.

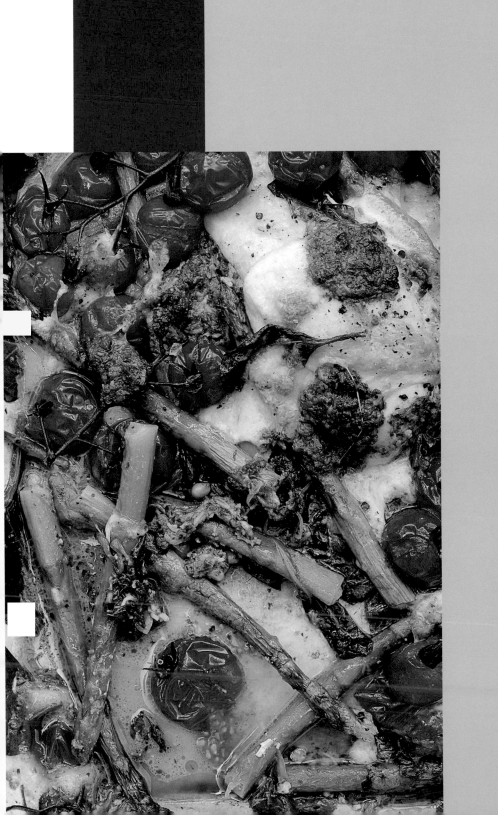

Spaghetti with pesto, peas and pancetta

Serves 4 adults

400g spaghetti
200g pancetta or bacon
  lardons or rashers
1 tsp olive oil
Handful of frozen peas
2 tbsp pesto
Salt and pepper

To serve

Basil leaves
Large handful of grated
  Parmesan cheese

Where would we be without pesto? Its position as storecupboard staple seems to have come from nowhere. We certainly didn't have it when we were growing up, but our children eat it like it's going out of fashion. Spaghetti and pancetta are its natural bedfellows.

1. Cook the spaghetti according to the packet instructions. While it is bubbling away, fry the pancetta or bacon in the oil until the fat has rendered and it is nice and crisp.

2. Four minutes before the spaghetti has finished cooking, add the peas to the cooking water.

3. When they're done, drain the spaghetti and the peas, reserving a couple of spoonfuls of cooking water.

4. Return the spaghetti and peas to the saucepan with the reserved cooking water, then add the pancetta, with all its lovely flavoursome oil, and the pesto. Mix well. Season, then garnish with a few basil leaves. Serve alongside a generous amount of Parmesan, for sprinkling.

Life-saving noodles

Serves 2 adults

Glug of garlic-infused oil
½ head of broccoli, divided
  into florets, or 1 pack of
  Tenderstem broccoli
12 large prawns, fresh or
  frozen, whatever you have
Good glug of soy sauce,
  plus more to serve
2 x 150g packs of
  straight-to-wok noodles
Sesame seeds (optional)

The ultimate fast food. A gorgeous prawn and broccoli noodle stir-fry that takes just seven minutes from start to on-the-plate. The noodles are bought part-cooked and are one of Mumsnet's favourite shortcuts.

Replace broccoli with sweetcorn for an even easier meal. And did you know prawns can be cooked from frozen? There is no need to defrost them, just make sure you heat them until they are cooked right through.

1. Put some garlic-infused oil in a wok or large frying pan over a medium heat, then add the broccoli florets, prawns and soy sauce.

2. Cook for about five minutes, stirring well, then add all the noodles. Cook for two more minutes or until the prawns and noodles are heated all the way through.

3. Sprinkle on some sesame seeds, if you want, stir and serve. Offer the bottle of soy sauce on the side, for those who want to add more.

Curried baked beans

Serves 2 adults

1 onion, chopped (or the
   equivalent in frozen
   chopped onion)
Glug of olive oil
2 garlic cloves,
   roughly chopped
2 tsp garam masala
½ tsp turmeric
1 tsp caster sugar
1cm piece of root
   ginger, grated
400g tin of chopped
   tomatoes
400g tin of haricot beans,
   drained and rinsed

To serve
Yogurt or crème fraîche
Chopped coriander leaves

 Vegetarian

✳ Freezable

Of course we're a fan of the real thing. Naked baked beans, accompanied by nothing more than a fork. And maybe a plate. However, sometimes you want beans with a little more flavour, a bit more punch, but that take no time to prepare. This is that dish. Despite the curry tag there is no heat, just fragrant flavours, so kids love it. It is perfect for everyone's lunch, the kids' tea or – if the cupboard is bare – your dinner.

If you want to make this dish even more quickly, forget about using a tin of haricot beans and a tin of tomatoes. Just open a couple of tins of normal baked beans. Obviously they already contain sugar, so leave that out of the recipe.

1. In a saucepan, gently fry the onion in the oil.

2. After a couple of minutes add the garlic, then the spices, sugar and ginger. Add the tomatoes and beans, bring to the boil, then reduce the heat and gently simmer for 10 minutes. Longer if you have it.

3. Serve in a bowl with yogurt or crème fraîche on the side and a bit of coriander sprinkled on top.

Lazy days couscous

Serves 6 adults as a side
dish or light lunch

250g couscous

350ml hot vegetable or
   chicken stock, or water

50g dried sour cherries
   (available in supermarket
   baking sections)

Glug of olive oil

50g unsalted shelled
   pistachio nuts

Salt and pepper

Generous squeeze of
   lemon juice

100g feta cheese, cubed
   or sliced

Handful of parsley leaves,
   finely chopped

❦ Vegetarian

Use vegetable stock, and
make sure the feta you
choose is vegetarian.

Couscous is a great alternative to break up the pasta, rice or potatoes routine. It is a real flavour magnet too and loves being dressed up with herbs and lemon juice. Here it is soaked (no cooking required, yay!) in stock and served with feta, sour cherries and pistachios (bear in mind that whole nuts can be a choking hazard; chop them or leave them out if your children are younger than five years old, see page 14). This is lovely with roast meats. The leftovers work perfectly for lunch boxes. Yours, not theirs.

1. Put the couscous in a large bowl and pour over the stock or water. Put a plate on top of the bowl and leave for five minutes.

2. Chop the sour cherries in half.

3. When all the stock has been absorbed by the couscous, fluff it up with a fork to separate the grains. Add the oil and stir it through, then add the pistachios and sour cherries. Mix and season with salt and pepper, then squeeze on some lemon juice. Arrange the feta cheese on top.

4. If eating straight away, add the parsley. If eating later, add the parsley just before serving (this means it will last longer in the fridge, so it's good to bear in mind if you're saving some for packed lunches).

Garlic mushrooms

Serves 2 adults

250g mushrooms
  – whatever you have, but
  it's quite nice to have a
  mix – say button, chestnut
  and portobello
Large knob of
  unsalted butter
75g (half a pack) garlic
  Boursin or other
  soft cheese
200g watercress or rocket
4 slices of crusty bread,
  toasted or griddled

❦ Vegetarian

Check the soft cheese you
use is vegetarian; not all of
them are.

♥ The health bit

Not only is this delicious and
obscenely easy, it's also really
good for you. Result! Gram
for gram, watercress contains
12 times more vitamin C than
lettuce *and* has more iron
than spinach. It's also rich
in several of the B vitamins,
as well as in betacarotene,
magnesium and potassium.
And it doesn't stop there, oh
no. Watercress also contains
a host of phytochemicals,
many of which have been
shown to have powerful
anti-cancer properties.

Sometimes, after a long, tiresome day, we have to accept that
our dinner is going to be toast. Don't cry. If it's toast with these
babies on it, you're laughing. Thick, meaty slices of mushroom
covered with a deliciously rich sauce mean this doesn't feel like
a poor substitute for an evening meal. Just add a glass of red wine
and dinner *est prêt*.

1. Trim the mushrooms, wash them if they look muddy – otherwise
don't bother – then slice them.

2. Melt the butter in a frying pan. Once it has melted, throw in the
mushrooms and fry them until they have softened and released most
of their water.

3. When the mushrooms look cooked, soft and wilted, remove from
the heat and stir in the Boursin. The juices will turn into a delicious and
aromatic sauce.

4. Serve on top of a bed of watercress or rocket on toast, seasoning well.
Pour yourself a large glass of red. You deserve it.

Italian baked chicken

Serves 2 adults

200g pack of spinach
450g asparagus spears
2 skinless chicken breasts
4 tsp pesto
125g mozzarella,
  torn into pieces
250g punnet of cherry
  tomatoes on the vine

Ooh la la! As they definitely don't say in Italy. This great dinner is *super-diddly-umptious* **[adj. delicious, Tuscan dialect]. Not only has it got** *oodles* **[Italian pron. uh-dlee-ess] of flavour, it is** *fastissimo* **[superlative, Sicilian dialect] to prepare. We say prepare, we mean arrange. Just arrange ingredients in nice dish, then place in oven. Then eat. Chow, bella.**

1. Preheat the oven to 200°C/fan 180°C/gas mark 6.

2. Fill an ovenproof dish with as much spinach as you can, then layer over the asparagus. Pop the chicken on top, then dollop the pesto and lay the mozzarella over them. Arrange the cherry tomatoes around.

3. Pop the whole lot in the oven for 25 minutes. Check after 20 minutes and, if the cheese is going a bit too brown, cover with foil.

4. Skewer the thickest part of a breast and check the juices run clear. If they have a trace of pink, cook for five minutes more, then check again. Season, then serve with pasta.

Origami fish

Serves 2 adults

2 fillets of fish (cod, salmon
   or coley), around 200g
   per person
Salt and pepper
2 tbsp soy sauce
1 tbsp sesame oil
1 tbsp rice wine
1 tsp brown sugar
2cm piece of root ginger,
   finely grated
1 garlic clove, crushed
1 red chilli, finely sliced
2 spring onions,
   finely sliced
Flavourless oil, such as
   vegetable oil, for greasing
   the foil
Coriander leaves, to serve

♥ The health bit

As we should eat at least two
portions of fish a week, this
dish is a winner. White fish is
high in protein and full of
vitamin B12 which helps
maintain a healthy immune
system. It's also low in fat,
which makes it an all-round
Good Thing.

We admit that this is not *really* origami. It's just folding a bit of foil, but we're trying to make this meal sound more complicated than it is. That way you won't feel embarrassed serving it to your friends for dinner. Without the origami element, it really is too easy: buy fish, jazz up with chilli, a bit of ginger and a few other staples, then pop it in the oven. White fish has a rather delicate flavour which some enjoy, though others can find it a bit bland. We think this dish is the perfect answer to both opinions.

1. Preheat the oven to 200°C/fan 180°C/gas mark 4.

2. Season the fish with salt and pepper. Make a sauce by combining the soy sauce, sesame oil, rice wine, sugar, ginger, garlic, most of the chilli and half the spring onions. Pour the sauce into a flat, non-metallic dish, place the fish in it and spoon the marinade over the top.

3. Cut two large squares of foil, each about 30cm. Place them on a baking tray. Oil their centres, then pop on the fish. Pull the sides of the foil up, so it creates a bowl shape, then divide the marinade between the parcels, spooning it on to the fish. Now loosely close the foil around the fish to make a 'tent', but scrunch the edges together to seal it completely. Put on a baking tray and bake in the hot oven for 15–20 minutes.

4. Take the parcels out of the oven and let them rest for five minutes. Either let your guests open their own parcels at the table (and get a great waft of aromatic steam as they do so), or plate the fish up first. Serve with noodles, the coriander and the remaining chilli and spring onions.

Mackerel pâté

Serves 4 adults

500g smoked mackerel
2 tbsp mayonnaise
Juice of 1 lemon, plus
   lemon wedges
   to serve (optional)
120g crème fraîche
Pepper
Chopped chives or parsley
   leaves (optional)
Toast, to serve

♥ **The health bit**

Smoked mackerel is rich in most of the B vitamins, particularly B12. It also provides good amounts of the mineral selenium, which is important for a healthy immune system.

This is great for lunch or tea, is whipped up in seconds, and kids love it. Suspend your disbelief (we can feel it from here) and follow these simple tips. Serve on wholemeal toast, place in front of child (no flinching or making faces, children will feel your fear) and back away from the table. It's a healthy meal made in minutes and you've made them cleverer with all those omega-3 fatty acids.

If you want to mix it up a bit, there's lots of things you can add to this pâté. A bit of horseradish is great, if you think your children's taste buds can take it. Stir in some chopped chives or finely sliced spring onions. Or, instead of crème fraîche, try cream cheese or a combination, depending on what you have in the fridge.

1. Peel the mackerel flesh from the skin (discard the skin) and flake the fish into a bowl, removing any bones you find as you do so.

2. Add the mayonnaise, lemon juice and crème fraîche, then mash thoroughly with a fork. Season with pepper.

3. Put the mix into a clean bowl and garnish with a bit of greenery if you have it; chives are perfect, parsley is nice. Cover and keep in the fridge until needed, or knock it up when there's five minutes until lunch time. Serve on hot toast, offering lemon wedges, if you like.

Simple soda bread

Makes 1 loaf

Flavourless oil, such
   as vegetable oil, for
   greasing the tray
125g plain flour
125g wholemeal flour
Salt
1 tsp bicarbonate of soda
2–3 tsp soft brown sugar
250ml buttermilk (or
   whole milk and 1 tbsp
   lemon juice, see right)

 Vegetarian

❋ Freezable

This recipe is beautiful in its simplicity. There is no kneading or proving, just a quick mix of all the ingredients followed by 30 minutes in a hot oven. It is the bread recipe for people who think they can't bake bread. You should have everything you need in your cupboard (there's *no yeast*!). OK, you may not have buttermilk, but you can easily make your own by mixing lemon juice with milk. (Stir 1 tbsp lemon juice into 250ml whole milk and let it stand for five minutes; it should look curdled.)

If you don't want the bread to have a hard crust, wrap the loaf in a clean tea towel shortly after taking it out of the oven. Eat it (or freeze it) as soon as possible. Normally it's wonderfully crumbly, though that means it's not great for toasting.

Wholemeal bread can be a hard sell for children, so be sneaky and introduce it slowly by gradually increasing the proportion of wholemeal to white flour. When baking with wholemeal flour alone, add a bit more liquid and a touch more bicarbonate of soda.

1. Preheat the oven to 230°C/fan 210°C/gas mark 8 and lightly oil a baking tray.

2. Pour both flours into a large bowl. Add 1 tsp of salt, the bicarbonate of soda, sugar and buttermilk and mix with a wooden spoon. Once it has come together, use your hands to form it into a ball shape. Squidge it down slightly with your palm, then take a sharp serrated knife and cut a deep cross in the top of the loaf.

3. Put on the oiled baking tray and place on the centre shelf of the oven to bake for around 12 minutes. Then reduce the oven temperature to 200°C/fan 180°C/gas mark 6 for 15 more minutes.

4. Using oven gloves, take the loaf out and give it a knock on its bottom. It is done if you hear a hollow sound. Cool on a wire rack.

60-second cheesecake

Makes... as many as you can before you're busted

❦ **Vegetarian**
Check the cream cheese you use is vegetarian; not all of them are.

---

1. Take one digestive biscuit.

2. Spread liberally with cream cheese.

3. Pop some blueberries, raspberries, or sliced strawberries on top. (They added poncey thyme leaves for the photo. There's no need for such fancy-pantedness in your own kitchen.)

4. Sift over some icing sugar.

5. Ta-da! A cheesecake.

6. Eat in one mouthful.

7. Glance over your shoulder to check no one saw.

8. Check for crumbs.

Cooking with Children

Top ten!

- **Taking the pizza**
- **Burger me!**
- **Chicken dippers**
- **Cheese and sweetcorn pancakes**
- **The jammiest of tarts**
- **Meringues**
- **One-pot fruity buns**
- **'I made them myself' biscuits**
- **Chocolate chip cookies**
- **Chocolate modelling dough**

Some things in life seem better in anticipation, or in the imagination. Parties are more fun, holidays more relaxing, dresses more flattering. And, in this spirit of honesty, cooking with children can fall into the same category.

The *idea* of baking delicious fairy cakes in family harmony – possibly while humming the theme tune to *The Waltons* – can fall some way short of the reality of sticky fingers over the walls and flour on the floor, to the theme tune of your children bickering.

After many batter-splodged afternoons in the kitchen with our children, we have realised that the secret of success is not to care too much about the end result. Expectations must be lowered. To the earth's molten core.

So relax and remember the fun is in the mixing and the mess, not in producing artisan grub. If the end result is edible – bonus! – but whiling away a rainy afternoon whilst potentially sowing the seeds for a life-long love affair with food is far more important.

If we sound like we are being preachy, we apologise. But this next sentence amply demonstrates why we care and why we think cooking is a fundamental life skill.

A survey of 2,000 people in 2012 showed that four in ten 16–23 year olds did *not* know milk came from a cow. One-third did not know that bacon comes from pigs. Seriously. While everyone here at Mumsnet Towers thinks a bacon tree sounds like a great idea, as processed foods become further entrenched in the nation's culinary vernacular, it is easy to see why basic cooking skills are declining.

The fact that you are reading this book probably means you realise they matter. Cooking well means eating well and, health benefits aside, ~~chocolate~~ good food is one of life's greatest pleasures. Sermon over.

It is amazing what children can achieve in the kitchen with a little supervision and a lot of encouragement. The entry level here is probably 'I made them myself' biscuits, closely followed by The jammiest of tarts. Children love cake and baking one is a good way to get them interested in making their own food. Weighing out ingredients and working out cooking times is a fun way to learn sums. There is near-immediate gratification.

Children are also more likely to try new savoury dishes if they have helped make them. The Chicken dippers are quick and healthy and loved by young and old alike. So are the burgers. As for pizza, if you teach your child to cook it, they will never go hungry again. When they eventually leave home, cooking a mean pizza is scientifically proven to boost their love lives. Come university, most students will bend over backwards for a free stuffed crust.

There is, of course, another motive. After all those years of slaving over a hot stove for your children, teaching them cooking skills could mean that one day – perhaps not too far in the future – they may return the favour.

But it is 100 per cent guaranteed that you will still be left with all the washing up.

Taking the pizza

Makes 2 medium-crust, 4 thin-crust, or lots of little pizzas

For the bases
450g strong white flour if you have it, plain if you don't, plus more to dust
Salt
7g (a little packet) fast-action yeast
1 tsp caster sugar
2 tsp olive oil, plus more for the bowl

For the sauce
¼–½ quantity Hands-off tomato sauce (see page 139)
or
Tomato purée

Suggested toppings
Pesto
Mini mozzarella balls
Grated mozzarella
Pepperoni
Sweetcorn
Ham
Cherry tomatoes
Basil leaves

❦ Vegetarian

✲ **Freezable**
The dough can be frozen before making the pizzas.

It used to be that pizza was fast food. Just whip it out of the freezer or call a takeaway. Not any more. Now you have children and make (some) things from scratch, pizza is a slower process. And if said children are going to help you? Allow even more time. But it's worth it. This base is light, fluffy and delicious. And kids adore every aspect of this meal, from the making to the eating, so it's a brilliant one to use as a bribe.

Older kids can help make the dough and turn it into pizza bases. Younger children can be given the bases with the tomato sauce on and add their own toppings. Letting kids do this always takes longer than you think. We recommend (from bitter experience) that you make one and have it in the oven while the children are putting toppings on theirs. That way they have something to eat once they've finished 'cooking' and there isn't 15 minutes of mayhem while they wait for their food.

Another top tip is to make one enormous pizza that covers an entire baking tray and get children to top their own quarter of it. That way you're not running backwards and forwards to the oven every few minutes.

1. Put the flour, 2 tsp of salt, the yeast and sugar in a large bowl and mix until everything is evenly distributed.

2. Make a well in the centre of the dry ingredients and pour in the olive oil and then 300ml of warm-to-the-touch water. Make sure the water is not too hot as that may kill the yeast. Mix it all together to form a dough, adding more water or flour if necessary.

3. Knead the dough on a floured work surface for five minutes.

4. Lightly oil a bowl, put the ball of dough inside and roll it around so each surface gets a light covering of oil to stop it drying out. Place a damp tea towel over it and leave the bowl to prove somewhere warm and draught-free until it doubles in size. After about an hour it should be ready, so take it out of the bowl. Turn the oven on as high as it will go and make sure you have a couple of shelves quite high up in the oven so you can fit in more than one pizza.

5. Now knock back the dough. This just involves giving it a light knead for 20–30 seconds, knocking out the air until it goes back to its original size. At this point you can freeze or refrigerate the dough until you need it.

6. Break off half the dough if you want a medium-crust pizza, one-quarter of the dough if you want a thin-crust pizza, less if you want smaller ones. If you are making thin-crust pizzas, roll it out as thin as you can on a floured surface. If you want a medium-crust pizza, don't roll it so thinly (d'oh!). Sometimes dough gets to a certain size and then keeps pinging back; if this happens, you can pull it about a bit with your hands to get a good 'pizza' shape.

7. Place the pizza base on a sheet of greaseproof paper. Smother it in tomato sauce, or purée straight from the tube does the trick. Or mix purée with a bit of pesto. Come on, you've made the base, you can cheat elsewhere! Add your favourite toppings.

8. When the oven is piping hot, open the door and pull out one of the shelves. Transfer the greaseproof paper and pizza directly on to the shelf, to give the pizza a crisper base.

9. Let the pizza cook for 10–12 minutes, until the dough is golden. Meanwhile get on with preparing the other pizzas.

Burger me!

Serves 4 adults

3–4 spring onions,
  finely chopped
1 tbsp flavourless oil,
  such as vegetable oil,
  plus more to cook
500g minced steak
2–3 handfuls of breadcrumbs
1 egg, lightly beaten
Salt and pepper

Some serving suggestions
Small baps
Tomato slices
Ketchup
Mayonnaise
Cheese slices
Shredded lettuce
Gherkins

✳ **Freezable**
As long as the meat was not
previously frozen, the raw
patties can be open-frozen in
a single layer, then transferred
to a freezer bag for storage.

♥ **The health bit**
With consumers ever more
watchful about what actually
goes into their burgers, it is
really worth making your own.
Get your butcher to grind the
meat in front of you if you want
to be extra sure of what it was
before it was mince...

Everyone loves a beef burger. Well, except vegetarians (and luckily they can try the delicious Bean burgers on page 121 instead). These are super-easy and not only can your kids help make the patties (just tidy them up a bit when they're not looking), but they can also customise their bun with a choice of fillings and condiments.

The list of ingredients in the burger mix is merely a suggestion. You could add grated Parmesan cheese, herbs, mustard, lemon zest... The condiment drawer is your oyster.

The only thing you really do need is good-quality minced steak. It isn't that expensive and has the perfect meat-to-fat ratio for a mean burger. It also freezes well, so buy some next time you go to the butcher and whip it out when you're after some red meat.

1. Gently fry the spring onions in the oil until they are translucent.

2. Put the minced meat in a bowl and add the cooked spring onions, breadcrumbs and egg, then season with salt and pepper. Stir well.

3. Once the kids have washed their hands they can take handfuls of the burger mix and make small patties. Make sure they're not too thick or they'll be raw on the inside and burned on the outside (yes, we admit it, we made them a bit too podgy for the photograph...). If you want to be fussy about it, make them slightly thinner in the middle, so when they cook they will be flat rather than domed. Get the kids to wash their hands thoroughly once more.

4. Heat a little more oil in a large frying pan over a medium heat. Add the burgers and fry for five to seven minutes on each side. Cut one in half and check to see how rare it is. When it is cooked to your liking, take off the heat.

5. Serve with baps, tomato slices, ketchup, mayonnaise, cheese slices and anything else you think you can sneak in. Some lettuce? Gherkins? Go on, try...

Chicken dippers

Serves 4 adults

450g skinless chicken
  breast, or the same weight
  of mini-fillets
150g crème fraîche
150g breadcrumbs
Salt and pepper
Flavourless oil, such as
  vegetable oil, to fry

✳ **Freezable**
As long as the chicken was
not previously frozen, the
crumb-coated raw dippers
can be open-frozen in a single
layer, then transferred to a
freezer bag for storage.

OK, OK, these are nuggets by any other name, but do give them a chance. Forget everything you've heard about that maligned food. Instead, think succulent chicken, dipped in perfectly seasoned breadcrumbs and lightly fried. This is a dish you'll be proud to serve to your kids.

We have it on good authority that instead of breadcrumbs you can use broken up Ritz crackers (Nigella) or Jacob's crackers (Jamie). We've also tried a 50:50 mixture of semolina and breadcrumbs which works well, as do cornflakes when given a bash with a rolling pin.

1. Slice the chicken breast so the dippers are about 7cm long and 2cm wide. Do try to keep them vaguely equal so the cooking time is the same for all of them. (Mini-fillets can be left as they are.)

2. Place the crème fraîche in a shallow container and the breadcrumbs in another. Add salt and pepper to the breadcrumbs.

3. Make your children wash their hands really well. Give them a piece of chicken and let them dip it first into the crème fraîche, then into the crumbs. It's very easy and quite satisfying. Place each finished dipper on a plate. Once the dippers have all been dipped, the children should wash their hands thoroughly again.

4. Heat enough oil to cover the base of a large frying pan. Place as many dippers in the frying pan as you can, without them touching each other. Cook for five minutes, until golden brown, then turn and fry for another four or five minutes. Cut the fattest one in half to check there is no trace of pink. If it's ready, remove the dippers from the pan on to kitchen paper and keep warm in an oven preheated to 150°C/fan 130°C/gas mark 2 while you cook the rest. If it isn't, cook for another minute, then test again. Repeat to cook all the dippers. You may have to increase or reduce the heat under the pan, especially for the subsequent batches, to get an even colour without scorching the dippers.

5. Serve up the rest of the meal – peas, mashed potato, ketchup (obv) – then put the dippers on the plate. Serve to deliriously happy children. And adults.

Cheese and sweetcorn pancakes

Makes about 8, depending on size

115g self-raising flour
½ tsp baking powder
Salt
¼ tsp mustard powder (optional)
55g Cheddar or other hard cheese, grated
200g tin of sweetcorn, drained and rinsed
1 egg
150ml milk
2 spring onions, finely sliced (optional)
Knob of unsalted butter

❦ **Vegetarian**
Make sure you choose a vegetarian cheese.

Show us a child that doesn't like cheese or sweetcorn and we will show you our One Direction memorabilia collection. These pancakes are not only beloved by children to eat, but also very easy for them to help to make. They are perfect for those days when lunch or tea takes you by surprise, as they are made from storecupboard essentials.

Older children can easily make these on their own. Maybe even for you! For tea! Younger children can do all the mixing and stirring by themselves (they are almost impossible to mess up), but will need a hand with the hot stuff.

1. Put the flour, baking powder, ¼ tsp of salt and the mustard powder in a large bowl (life is too short to sift), then stir in the cheese and sweetcorn.

2. Lightly beat the egg and milk together in a mug, jug or small bowl, then gently stir into the flour mixture to form a thick batter. If you want to spice it up a bit, fry the spring onions (borrowing a bit of your knob of butter) and add them to the batter.

3. Place the batter in the fridge for an hour or so (less in a food-related emergency) to thicken up.

4. Melt the butter in a large frying pan over a medium heat until it is bubbling. Drop large spoonfuls of the batter into the pan. Make sure you space them well apart, as they have a habit of spreading and jostling one another. You will probably have to cook them in batches. Cook for about three minutes, then flip over for another three minutes until they are golden brown and crisp. Place on kitchen paper and keep warm in a single layer in an oven preheated to 150°C/fan 130°C/gas mark 2 while you cook the rest. You may have to increase or reduce the heat under the frying pan, especially for the subsequent batches, to avoid scorching any of the pancakes.

5. Serve with brown sauce or, if you have the time and energy, these are delicious with some finely chopped avocado and tomato.

The jammiest of tarts

Makes 12

225g plain flour,
  plus more to dust
110g unsalted butter,
  plus more for the tray
25g caster sugar
2 egg yolks
Salt
Lemon curd or jam (any
  flavour, using different
  colours looks lovely)
A little milk, to glaze

☛ **You will need**
Fairy cake tray; 8cm biscuit
cutter; small heart, star or
other fun cutter.

❦ **Vegetarian**

❊ **Freezable**
The pastry is freezable
before baking.

Mumsnet likes a campaign and this is our most fervent to date. For too long, jam tarts have been in baked goods exile. We want them to receive the recognition they deserve. Our children are suffering! So we are campaigning for their return to the spotlight. These ones are easy to make (yes, even the pastry). They are jammy. They are tarty. They are a million miles away from shop-bought impostors. Justice for jam tarts starts here.

Little ones can help roll out the pastry, cut out the shapes and fill the tarts with jam. Be careful when the tarts come out of the oven… they will be extremely hot but very tempting, especially to little lips!

1. Whizz the flour, butter, sugar, egg yolks and a pinch of salt together in a food processor until the mixture comes together into a ball. If it is a bit crumbly, add a little water. If you don't have a food processor, rub the butter into the flour, sugar and salt in a bowl until the mixture resembles breadcrumbs, then add water and bring it together into a ball.

2. Wrap the ball in cling film and pop in the fridge for 30 minutes, so it chills slightly before rolling.

3. Butter a fairy cake tray and preheat the oven to a temperature of 180°C/fan 160°C/gas mark 4.

4. Take your pastry out of the fridge, dust a work top and rolling pin with some flour and roll out the pastry so it is about 4mm thick. You don't need to get your ruler out, just guess.

5. Using an 8cm biscuit cutter (the perfect size for your average jam tart) cut the pastry into circles.

6. Pop the circles into the fairy cake tin and push each one down so it fits snugly. Plop a dollop of lemon curd or jam in each one, not too much as it will bubble up. Using a small cutter, cut out pastry hearts, stars or, if you are a particularly nice parent, your children's initials, using leftover pastry. Pop one on each jam tart and brush the pastry bits with milk.

7. Bake for 15–20 minutes, until the edges of the tarts are golden. Lift on to a wire rack to cool. Quickly stuff two in your gob, whilst 'tidying the cupboard under the stairs' and tell your children that, sadly, a couple burnt. Wipe away the crumbs.

Meringues

Makes 8–12,
depending on size

3 egg whites (bottled egg
  whites are brilliant as they
  solve the leftover yolk
  conundrum)
175g caster sugar

 Vegetarian

Meringues are notorious: supposedly too difficult for the home cook to master. The glory of the cloud-like confections tricks people into a panic. But we will let you into a secret. These are so easy, children can make them with little or no supervision. Some other recipes include cornflour or vinegar, but these are crisp, gooey-centred meringues without bothering with either.

They are particularly delicious when crumbled and mixed with cream whipped with a spoon of icing sugar and some chopped strawberries (a traditional Eton mess) or, if you're feeling totally tropical, some chopped pineapple and passion fruit.

1. Preheat the oven to 140°C/fan 120°C/gas mark 1. Line a baking sheet with non-stick baking parchment (meringues will stick to greaseproof paper) or a silicone sheet.

2. Whisk the egg whites in a large clean, dry bowl until they form soft peaks. An electric whisk is by far the quickest way to do this, although littler children may prefer using a balloon whisk as it is less noisy. The whisked egg white is ready when you can turn the bowl upside down over your head without getting egg in your hair.

3. Add the caster sugar a dessertspoonful at a time, whisking in each addition thoroughly, until it is all gone and the meringue mixture is thick, glossy and smooth, not granular.

4. Spoon blobs of the mixture on to the baking parchment. If they are for something special, draw around the bottom of a cup and use that as a size guide, so they are all even. Leave a small space between each meringue.

5. Place the sheet in the oven and cook for one hour. Then turn the oven off and leave them in there until it is completely cold, ideally overnight.

One-pot fruity buns

Makes 12

150g (small pot)
  of natural yogurt
1 small yogurt pot
  of caster sugar
3 small yogurt pots
  of self-raising flour
1 small yogurt pot
  of sunflower oil
3 eggs, lightly beaten
Finely grated zest of
  1 unwaxed lemon
½ small yogurt pot
  of sultanas

☛ **You will need**
Fairy cake tray; 12 fairy
cake cases.

♥ **Vegetarian**

These buns can be made more or less entirely without adult intervention. You don't even need scales, as ingredients are measured out in a yogurt pot. It is a great way of giving children independence in the kitchen. They are light and fluffy and best eaten on the day they are made.

1. Preheat the oven to 180°C/fan 160°C/gas mark 4. Line a fairy cake tray with fairy cake cases.

2. Pour the pot of natural yogurt into a bowl. Rinse and dry the pot and use it to measure out the sugar, flour and oil (in that order) into the bowl. Add the eggs and mix everything together until you have a light batter, then tip in the lemon zest and sultanas. Give it another good stir.

3. Spoon the batter into the cake cases and bake for 15 minutes. When the buns are golden brown, they are done. Transfer them to a wire rack to cool and eat them up quickly.

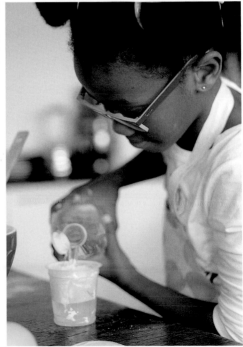

'I made them myself' biscuits

Makes about 20

125g dark brown sugar
125g unsalted butter, well
    softened, cut into cubes
1 egg
Few drops of vanilla extract
250g plain flour, plus more
    to dust

To decorate (optional)
50–100g icing sugar
A little lemon or
    beetroot juice
Sprinkles, or other
    sugar decorations

☞ **You will need**
Biscuit cutters.

❦ **Vegetarian**

❄ **Freezable**
The biscuit dough can be
frozen before cooking.

These are really easy to make and almost impossible to destroy. Toddlers may maul, pre-schoolers may lick, and you may not choose to offer the most man-handled biscuits to a guest – though 180 degrees of heat should kibosh any introduced germs from under fingernails – but the chances are they will all *look* OK.

1. Put the sugar and butter in a bowl and cream, using an electric mixer or a wooden spoon (takes a bit longer but does wonders for upper body strength). Break the egg into a cup or small bowl, add the vanilla extract, beat lightly with a fork, then slowly add to the butter and sugar, mixing all the time.

2. Add the flour and mix it in until you've got a dough ball. Wrap it in cling film, then pop it in the fridge for 20 minutes (or more, in which case it may get a bit hard, so just take it out of the fridge and let it warm up a bit before you try to roll it out).

3. Line two baking trays with greaseproof paper and preheat the oven to 180°C/fan 160°C/gas mark 4.

4. When the dough is ready, sprinkle some flour on a work surface and, using a rolling pin, roll out the dough to about 5mm thick.

5. This is when the kids can really get involved. With clean hands they can cut the biscuits into a variety of shapes, using children's knives and biscuit cutters. Then put them on the baking trays and bake for 10–12 minutes. Remove, leave on the trays for a couple of minutes, then transfer to a wire rack with a palette knife. Leave to cool.

6. Knock together a very basic icing, if you want, by sifting the icing sugar into a large bowl and mixing in the juice: lemon juice tastes lovely, while beetroot juice makes a bright pink but doesn't taste of beetroot. You just need enough juice to get the icing to the right consistency.

7. Once the biscuits have cooled, you can spread a little icing over them, then decorate them with the sprinkles and allow to dry and set.

Chocolate chip cookies

Makes 8-ish cookies

175g plain flour
½ tsp bicarbonate of soda
Salt
110g unsalted butter, well softened, plus more for the tray
85g caster sugar
90g soft brown sugar
½ tsp vanilla extract
1 egg, lightly beaten
175g dark chocolate chips

❤ Vegetarian

❄ Freezable
The dough can be frozen before cooking.

There is nothing closer to a Mumsnetter's heart than biscuits. We'll eat anything really. Jammy dodgers, custard creams, garibaldis – but these chocolate chip cookies really take the biscuit. They are crisp with a chewy middle and are a massive sugar-hit for both children and adults.

You can serve them straight from the oven, with a scoop of vanilla ice cream sandwiched between the two. Or so we have been told...

1. In a large bowl, mix the flour, bicarbonate of soda and ½ tsp of salt.

2. In another bowl, using an electric mixer, beat the butter, caster sugar, brown sugar and vanilla extract until creamy.

3. Mix in the egg, then gradually add the flour mixture. When it is all nicely combined, stir in the chocolate chips.

4. Lay a large piece of cling film on your work surface. Put the dough in the middle in a sausage shape. Roll while twiddling each end, so all the dough is encased in cling film, a bit like a cracker. Gently roll the dough under your palms (still in the cling film) on the work surface, to make the sausage evenly-shaped. Pop it in the fridge to harden up for 30 minutes.

5. Preheat the oven to 190°C/fan 170°C/gas mark 5 and butter two baking trays.

6. Unwrap the cookie dough sausage and slice it 2cm thick. Lay these discs on the baking trays, spacing each well (and we mean *well*) away from the next. These cookies spread loads when baked. Cook for about 10 minutes, or until golden and hard on top. Remove, leave on the trays for a couple of minutes, then transfer to a wire rack with a palette knife. Leave to cool. Maybe.

Chocolate modelling dough

**Makes enough for
2 children**

250g plain flour
50g cocoa powder
125g old-fashioned table
 salt, *not* sea salt flakes
15g cream of tartar (find
 it in the baking aisle)
1 tbsp oil

**This stuff may smell good enough to eat but *don't eat it*!
As well as a healthy scoop of cocoa powder, this contains
125g of salt... bleurgh! Once you've got over the temptation,
you're laughing. This takes minutes to knock up and will
keep kids busy for, literally, minutes. It is the perfect response
to a rainy afternoon.**

1. Put the kettle on. Sift the flour and cocoa powder into a medium-sized
saucepan. Add the salt and cream of tartar. Stir in the oil along with
500ml of boiling water.

2. Place the saucepan over a medium-low heat, stirring all the while,
for one to four minutes, or until the dough solidifies. Stick your finger
into the dough. When it comes out clean, the dough is ready.

3. Let the dough cool, then take it out of the pan and knead until
it's smooth.

4. Result? Parent-free fun! Sit back, relax and enjoy the chocolatey aroma.

Party Time

Top ten!

- **Marmite swirls**
- **Sandwich nirvana**
- **Rock 'n' sausage roll**
- **Raspberry jam chicken**
- **Ice-cream-cone cakes**
- **The perfect chocolate cake**
- **Heavenly chocolate tray-bake**
- **Party toffee popcorn**
- **Icing**
- **Aunt Jura's home-made lemonade**

Children's parties are as complicated as you want them to be. Of course, you can hand-sew each child an individual party bag, personalise biscuits with guests' initials and spend a week constructing the perfect birthday cake. But equally you can replace the party bag with a pile of Mr Men books, serve chocolate fingers and buy a beautiful cake from the supermarket. Truth be told, as long as there's crisps, cakes and biscuits, no one under ten will care. And this chapter is aimed mainly at those primary school-aged children. In our experience, older children's parties are more about sleepovers and cinema trips.

So put your feet up, relax and follow Mumsnet's guide to fuss-free children's party catering.

First of all let's talk fripperies. Themed plates, napkins and cups are generally a rip off. White paper plates with a colourful napkin on top (a certain Swedish furniture store does excellent ones very reasonably) look just as good for half the price. Cartons of juice are quicker and less messy than cups filled by a jug.

OK, the food. Follow our guide in this chapter for sandwich-making tips, although no one will think twice if you serve Rock and sausage rolls, cheese and tomato pizza squares and Raspberry jam chicken instead, or as well. Sausage rolls and chicken can be prepared the night before and everything can be cooked on the day, ideally while the children play games or watch the entertainer.

Potato rings are essential (and no, they haven't got smaller, your fingers have got bigger). Obviously it's better to avoid anything with nuts, including chocolate spread. You can put out small bowls of cherry tomatoes and cucumber and carrot sticks, but we all know they are there just to impress the other parents. None of the children will touch them. Instead put some halved grapes out with the sandwiches and crisps 'course'. Children won't look twice at them if served with the cakes, but will eat them if they think it is the only sweet thing they are getting.

If you are going to do biscuits *and* cakes, the rule is to make one and buy in the other. Luridly-iced number-shaped biscuits are always a big hit and fairy cakes are massively popular, especially when they're doused with sprinkles. Did you know you can buy them in packs of 20 from the supermarket, ready to be iced, so they look 'home-made'? Shhhhh! Don't tell everyone. The last time we tried to buy some was the night before a school bake sale and our local supermarket had run out.

When the party is not at home, make sure you pack loads of kitchen paper, a knife to cut the cake and matches to light the candles.

And if you want to make your children very happy, conjure up a batch of jelly and fill it with slithery snake sweets (see page 278 for a photo) or gobstopper eyeballs. Revolting to look at, this is easy to make and can be whipped up the night before.

A final word of warning. It may sound a good idea to invite parents to stay, but remember that it'll mean providing cakes for the grown-ups and probably fizzy wine and beer, too. Whatever you do, *never* offer tea. Boiling a kettle, finding decent mugs and the right kind of tea bags, milk and sugar whilst dealing with 30 screaming children is no laughing matter.

When it is all over, breathe a big sigh of relief and crack open the wine. Only 364 more sleeps until the next one…

Marmite swirls

Makes about 10

250g (half a pack) of
  puff pastry
Plain flour, to dust
1 tsp Marmite
1 tsp unsalted butter,
  well softened
1 egg, lightly beaten
50g Cheddar or other hard
  cheese, grated
Flavourless oil, such as
  vegetable oil, for greasing
  the tray

❦ Vegetarian

✳ Freezable
The swirls can be frozen
before baking, if the pastry
has not been pre-frozen.
Open-freeze them in a single
layer, then transfer to a
freezer bag for storage.

Even people who don't like Marmite (*fools!*) will like these. They are very savoury, slightly cheesy pastries which have a delicious Marmitey tang. Cheese and Marmite is one of the culinary world's most overlooked flavour combinations. Move over cheese and pickle.

1. Take the pastry out of the fridge about 30 minutes before you use it. Preheat the oven to 230°C/fan 210°C/gas mark 8.

2. On a floured work surface, roll out the pastry into a rough rectangle. It should be about as thick as a one pound coin. Mix the Marmite with the butter and, using the back of the teaspoon, spread the mixture all over the pastry, leaving a 2cm border all the way around. Lick the spoon. Shiver. Brush the pastry edges with the beaten egg and then sprinkle the cheese all over the Marmite and butter mixture, leaving the border clear.

3. Roll the pastry tightly as if it were a Swiss roll. Cut it into 2cm-thick slices and place on a lightly oiled baking tray. Bake for 12–15 minutes until risen and golden, then transfer to a wire rack to cool. Eat warm or cold.

Sandwich nirvana

There is an art to the humble sandwich. We kid you not. It isn't just a case of slapping some butter on two pieces of bread and bunging a slice of ham in the middle. There is a big difference between a humdrum sandwich and the Truly Great Sandwich. Here are some of the basics.

- The butter *has* to be soft.

- Crusts should be cut off once the bread has been buttered and the sandwich made. If that sounds like a bit too much hassle, then most supermarkets sell crustless bread.

- Small children like sandwiches cut into shapes with biscuit cutters. Hearts or circles work better than stars (too pointy!).

- Take some finger-rolls, halve them, butter, then spread with your filling of choice. Stick flags made out of cocktail sticks in the top, and you have mini-boats.

- Always use butter or mayonnaise. It acts as a barrier and protects the filling from making the bread soggy. If the sandwiches are made in advance, avoid tomato and tuna because these also lead to sogginess.

- Children love jam sandwiches.

- Children love sprinkle sandwiches.

- Children love crisp sandwiches.

- Don't serve all three at the same party. People will assume your children have scurvy.

- Smoked salmon and cream cheese, ham and Cheddar, chicken and mayonnaise all go down well.

- Marmite sandwiches are one of life's joys. But do yourself a favour and mix equal amounts of Marmite and softened butter before spreading.

- Older children like making their own wraps. Put out bowls of houmous, sweetcorn, grated cheese and carrot and let them get on with it.

- If all that sounds like a faff, opt out and cook pizza squares and mini sausages instead.

Rock 'n' sausage roll

Makes 12 small rolls

Sheet of ready-rolled
  puff pastry, about 320g
Glug of flavourless oil,
  such as vegetable oil
1 red onion, finely chopped
6 sausages, or
  400g sausagemeat
1 tsp thyme leaves
Salt and pepper
1 egg, lightly beaten

✳ **Freezable**
The sausage rolls can be
frozen before baking, if the
pastry hasn't been pre-frozen.
Open-freeze in a single layer,
then transfer to a freezer bag
for storage.

Have you ever met a child who doesn't like sausages? Didn't think so. Which means we don't need to explain the popularity of these buttery bundles of deliciousness. Sarnies are left untouched, even crisps are shunned when these pastry pockets of delectability are on the table. That's if they make it to the table...

1. Take the pastry out of the fridge about 30 minutes before you use it. Preheat the oven to 180°C/fan 160°C/gas mark 4. Line a baking tray with greaseproof paper.

2. Put the oil in a pan and fry the red onion slowly until it is soft and slightly browned. Leave to cool while you remove the sausages from their skins and put the meat in a bowl. Or just put the sausagemeat in a bowl.

3. Once the onions are cool, mix them well into the sausagemeat. Add the thyme and salt and pepper and mix these in, too.

4. Place the pastry in front of you, in a landscape rather than portrait position. Cut it in half, vertically, and place half the sausage mix lengthways down the centre of each rectangle. With a pastry brush, paint the long edges of each with the egg. Then push the painted pastry edges of the first rectangle towards each other and crimp them using your finger and thumb, so they fix together. Do the same to the second rectangle of pastry.

5. With a sharp knife, cut each large sausage roll into six smaller ones. Stab (not too violently) the top of each roll two or three times so steam can come out. Place the rolls on the prepared baking tray, then paint with the remaining egg.

6. Pop the sausage rolls in the oven for about 30 minutes (keep an eye on them). When you take them out they should look golden and smell delicious. Try one, just in case.

Raspberry jam chicken

Serves 4 adults

3 tbsp raspberry jam
1 tsp red wine vinegar
2 tbsp soy sauce
½ tsp English mustard
1 garlic clove, crushed
4 skinless boneless
  chicken thighs

Yes, we really *are* suggesting marinating chicken pieces in raspberry jam. On reflection, it is not really as far-fetched as it sounds. After all, many marinades contain sugar. Plus raspberry jam is not a million miles away from cranberry jelly, and no one bats an eye at that combination. Anyway, adding red wine vinegar helps to cut through the sweetness. This recipe creates a really sticky, red chicken that children seem to love. Just a word of warning, don't skip lining your roasting tray or you'll be crowbarring burnt jam off it for weeks. Simply scale up the quantities, according to the number of guests.

1. Mix the jam, vinegar, soy sauce and mustard with the garlic in a saucepan and bring to the boil (careful though; boiling jam is super-hot). Remove the saucepan from the heat and allow the jam marinade to cool; it should be nice and gloopy.

2. When it is cool, tip the marinade into a non-metallic bowl (or into a sturdy freezer bag) and add the chicken pieces, rubbing in the marinade thoroughly. The longer you marinate it for, the tastier it will be, but don't fret if you only have an hour or so. If you have longer, cover the bowl – or seal the bag and put it in a bowl in case of drips – and place in the fridge.

3. Preheat the oven to 180°C/fan 160°C/gas mark 4 and return the chicken to room temperature if it has been in the fridge. Line a roasting tray with greaseproof paper and tip the chicken on to the tray. Bake for about 30 minutes, turning once and watching closely towards the end of cooking time, as the pieces tend to catch if you are not careful.

ICE CREAM
FOR SALE

50p

Ice-cream-cone cakes

Makes 10

For the cakes
100g self-raising flour
100g caster sugar
100g unsalted butter,
  well softened
2 eggs, lightly beaten
½ tsp baking powder
10 flat-bottomed ice cream
  cones (available from
  any supermarket)

To decorate
1 quantity Buttercream
  icing (see page 258)
Sprinkles, sweets or glacé
  cherries
10 chocolate flakes
  (optional)

☛ **You will need**
Muffin tray.

❦ **Vegetarian**

This confection might just make your kid's year. It's a combination of all their favourite things: icing, cake, ice-cream cones. Put some sprinkles on top, maybe a flake and *bam*... your child has just exploded with joy.

1. Preheat the oven to 180°C/fan 160°C/gas mark 4.

2. Put all the cake ingredients in a large bowl (not the ice cream cones!). Using an electric whisk, mix until combined; the batter should look light and fluffy.

3. Wrap each cone in foil to prevent the mixture spilling on to the outside and to stop the cones from scorching in the oven. Spoon the mixture into each cone until it is about half full.

4. Place the cones in a muffin tray, to stop them falling over, and bake for 15–20 minutes until the cakes are golden and spring back to the touch. Once cooked, remove the foil.

5. Wait until the cakes have cooled, then ice with buttercream (pipe it on in ice-cream-van-style swirls, if you're feeling ambitious). Add sprinkles, sweets or glacé cherries, and even a Flake, if you're feeling generous.

The perfect chocolate cake

Makes 8 adult slices

For the cake
175g unsalted butter, well softened, plus more for the tins
1½ tbsp cocoa powder
175g self-raising flour
1½ tsp baking powder
175g caster sugar
3 eggs, lightly beaten

For the filling
3 tbsp raspberry or strawberry jam
Maltesers
or
284ml pot of double cream, whipped
About 150g raspberries

For the decoration
75–100g milk chocolate
Sprinkles or sweets

☛ **You will need**
2 x 18cm round cake tins.

❦ **Vegetarian**

A party would not be a party without chocolate cake. This one is our favourite. It is chocolately enough to sate even the most hormonal of mothers, but not overpoweringly rich, making it a hit with little people. Scattered with sweets, or sandwiched with whipped cream and raspberries, it can even take centre stage. All that's missing is some candles.

1. Preheat the oven to 180°C/fan 160°C/gas mark 4. Butter two 18cm sandwich tins and line the bases with greaseproof paper.

2. Using a spoon or fork, blend together the cocoa powder with 3 tbsp of hot water in a cup until there are no lumps. Once cool, beat the cocoa mixture into the remaining cake ingredients in a large bowl. If you have an electric mixer or a blender you can blitz everything in this instead.

3. Divide the mixture between the two prepared tins and bake in the oven for 25 minutes. When the cakes are cooked, put them on a wire rack in their tins until they are cool enough to handle, then turn out of the tins on to the rack, peel off the papers and leave to cool completely.

4. Put the least nice-looking cake on a serving plate, flat-side up, spread on some jam and Maltesers and then put the other cake on top, flat side facing the ceiling. Or spread the base cake with whipped cream and arrange on the raspberries before adding the top layer.

5. Use the milk chocolate to make a batch of Melted chocolate icing (see page 256), then chill it for 10 minutes, as directed.

6. And now for the fun part... decorating the cake. Spoon the icing over the cake, starting in the centre and allowing the chocolate to cascade down. Add sprinkles or sweets before it sets. If your kitchen is hot, put the cake in the fridge until the icing hardens up.

Heavenly chocolate tray-bake

Makes 15 small slices

170g golden syrup
225g unsalted butter
100g caster sugar
70g cocoa powder
350g digestive biscuits
50g dried cranberries
50g glacé cherries
50g unsalted shelled
  pistachio nuts

☛ **You will need**

30 x 23cm tray-bake tin,
or a small roasting tin.

❧ **Vegetarian**

This is perfect when you need a job-lot of cake. Two batches and you've done the whole class. If you don't have the correct ingredients, just vary the dried fruit and nut content, but keep the quantities the same. You don't even need a working oven as this is a refrigerator cake. And it's quick; no icing required. Really, we couldn't make it easier. Or more gooey. Or chocolatey. Or delicious. And without wanting to sound cheap, it's cheap, because you use cocoa powder and sugar instead of chocolate.

We've used cranberries, glacé cherries and pistachios here, but we're just showing off. Raisins, sultanas, whatever you've got is absolutely fine. That way you may even be able to make this without a trip to the shops. Just don't use whole nuts if serving it to children less than five years old (see page 14).

1. Line a 30 x 23cm tray-bake tin or a similarly sized small roasting tin with greaseproof paper.

2. Put the golden syrup, butter, sugar and cocoa powder in a saucepan over a medium heat and melt until smooth, stirring occasionally.

3. While the chocolate mixture is melting, put the biscuits in a plastic bag, exclude the air and tie the top of the bag. Get a rolling pin – or any other blunt instrument – and give the bag a good whack (children love doing this bit). You want to break up the biscuits into lots of little bits, but don't go so far as to pulverise it as you would for cheesecake.

4. When the chocolate mixture has melted, take it off the heat. Put the biscuit chunks, fruits and nuts in a large bowl. Pour the chocolate mixture over it and stir well.

5. Once everything is well covered in chocolate, turn the mix into the lined tin and flatten with the back of a spoon. Put a sheet of greaseproof paper over the mix, then place some heavy items on top, such as jam jars. Pop the whole thing in the fridge and allow it to set. It takes at least an hour.

6. Remove the tray-bake from the tin and peel off the papers, then cut it lengthways into three and widthways into five. That way you have made 15 small slices and cannot be blamed for the obesity epidemic in your immediate neighbourhood.

Party toffee popcorn

Serves 4 adults (makes 10 kid-sized handfuls)

3 tbsp flavourless oil, such as vegetable oil
75g popcorn kernels
25g unsalted butter
4 tbsp brown sugar
3 tbsp golden syrup

For cheesy popcorn
3 tbsp flavourless oil, such as vegetable oil
75g popcorn kernels
25g unsalted butter
Parmesan or other hard cheese, finely grated
Pinch of cayenne pepper (optional)
Pepper (optional)

❦ Vegetarian
Avoid Parmesan for vegetarian popcorn.

Bowls of fluffy popcorn are low on effort, but high on impact. Bring them out after the sarnies and watch them disappear. Kids of all ages like this, as do most adults. Make a bit extra and hand it out to any adult helpers who look like they need an energy boost. Goes very well with a glass of sparkly. Or apple juice.

1. Heat the oil in a large pan with a lid. Throw the popcorn into the pan and put the lid on. Wait and, after a minute or so, you'll hear the popping start. Give the pan a good shake and eventually the popping will stop. Take the pan off the heat immediately; you don't want the kernels to burn, since taking out individual burned bits of popcorn is not only labour intensive but also intensely annoying.

2. Empty the popcorn into a colander.

3. In the pan, melt the butter, then add the sugar and golden syrup. Let it mix and sizzle for a bit, then pour the popcorn back into the pan and remove from the heat. Put the lid back on and bang it about a bit so the popcorn mixes evenly with the toffee topping.

To make cheesy popcorn

Make the popcorn up to the point of emptying it into the colander (so up to the end of step 2). Now melt the butter in the pan, return the popcorn and remove from the heat. Straight away, sprinkle the cheese and cayenne or pepper on top (cayenne is best avoided for small children). Put the lid on and bang the pan about to coat the popcorn well with the cheesy mixture, then serve.

Icing

Let's face it, kids don't eat cakes because they like cake. They eat cakes because they *love* icing. How often have you found the sludgy remains of birthday cake, discarded because all the icing has been sucked off? Exactly. So Mary Berry may talk about the 'crumb', but when you're cooking cakes for kids, it's all about the icing. Here are our recipes and top tips for getting it right.

♥ **Vegetarian**

Melted chocolate icing

This is less chocolate icing and more just (ahem) chocolate. Melted. Yum. Super-easy, and loved by everyone. Use chocolate from the baking aisle, no one will know the difference, but avoid white chocolate as it doesn't melt in the same way. A regular 100g bar of chocolate will cover a 20cm cake, or 12 fairy cakes, with a bit left over for baker's perks.

Melting in a microwave: Break the chocolate into chunks in a glass bowl and pop it in the microwave on medium power for short bursts of 30 seconds, stirring in between. Stop when the chocolate is nearly melted, but there are still a few lumps visible. The heat of the melted chocolate will melt those last bits and, this way, you don't risk scorching the chocolate.

Melting in a bain-marie: More washing up than a microwave, but just as effective. Melt chunks of chocolate in a heatproof bowl suspended over a saucepan of lightly simmering water. The bowl mustn't touch the water. When it is glossy and smooth, it's ready.

To ice the cake: Let the melted chocolate cool down in the fridge for about 10 minutes. Then, using a spoon, pour the chocolate into the centre of the cake and let gravity take its course. Then let it harden, in the fridge if your kitchen is hot.

**Makes enough for
12 fairy cakes**

110g unsalted butter,
  well softened
320g icing sugar
2–3 tbsp single cream
  or milk
1 tsp vanilla extract
Food colourings (optional)

❤ Vegetarian

Buttercream icing

You know those towering cupcakes with scary amounts of icing? That's buttercream icing, or frosting as our US friends would call it. Intimidating to look at, this is actually very easy to make.

1. Put the butter in a large bowl. Using an electric whisk, churn it up.

2. Slowly whisk in the icing sugar, a bit at a time. Once all of the icing sugar has been added, pour in the cream or milk. It's at this point the mixture will start to look more like icing. Add vanilla extract and any food colouring that you want.

3. Apply to the cakes with a knife or the back of a spoon, or use a piping bag if you're feeling a bit arty.

**Makes enough for
6 fairy cakes or biscuits**

100g icing sugar,
  plus more if needed
1 tbsp lemon juice,
  orange juice or water,
  plus more if needed
Food colourings or
  beetroot juice (optional)

❤ Vegetarian

Glacé icing

Very easy, and probably what biscuits and fairy cakes were decorated with in your childhood… ahh, innocent times. These are perfect when adorned with lots and lots of sprinkles.

1. Sift the icing sugar (one of the rare times that you really need to sift something) into a large bowl and stir in the juice or water. The icing should coat the back of a spoon. If it's too liquid add more sugar; too stiff, add more juice. Easy.

2. Every supermarket sells liquid food colouring, which is simple to use. Just add a few drops to the icing. The more you add, the stronger the colour (but the thinner the icing will become, so take care). There are natural alternatives. A few drops of beetroot juice (just let some drops fall out of one of those vacuum packs of cooked beetroot; make sure it isn't in vinegar!) will turn icing pale pink; add more and it'll turn a glorious magenta colour, but crucially have no beetroot flavour.

**Makes enough for
a large cake**

50g unsalted butter
25g cocoa powder
2 tbsp milk
225g icing sugar

❤ Vegetarian

Chocolatey fudgey icing

This makes enough icing to sandwich two layers of sponge together and cover the cake, too. Decorate your iced cake with anything from Maltesers to chocolate buttons.

1. Melt the butter in a pan over a low heat, then stir in the cocoa powder and cook for one minute more.

2. Remove the pan from the heat and stir in the milk and icing sugar. Beat well and allow to cool a little before icing the cake.

Tips!

- **The sprinkles/hundreds and thousands conundrum:** You say hundreds and thousands, we say sprinkles... actually it doesn't matter which one you go for, more is more when it comes to embellishment. A good technique for covering a fairy cake is to fill a saucer with sprinkles, up-end the iced cake into the saucer and press gently.

- **Never underestimate the power of a penny sweet:** A sugar shrimp or cola cube on a fairy cake looks really good. A gummy bear, jelly baby or chocolate bunny may cause a riot. You've been warned.

- **More chocolate:** So you iced the cake in chocolate. Now put more chocolate on it. Using a vegetable peeler, make some chocolate curls. Add chocolate buttons. Maybe an actual large chunk of chocolate? It's impossible to go overboard.

- **Fruit:** A perfectly posed raspberry looks gorgeous on a chocolate fairy cake. It's just possible that adults will appreciate this one more than children...

Aunt Jura's home-made lemonade

Makes lots (about 2 litres of cordial)

3 unwaxed lemons
    (or 2 lemons and 2 limes)
900g caster or granulated
    sugar (yes, 900g!!)
30g citric acid (available
    from chemists)
Sprigs of mint, frozen
    raspberries and ice,
    to serve

 Vegetarian

We're not sure who Aunt Jura is (we suspect that she is a relative of Just William, or someone who lived up the Magic Faraway Tree), but we have her to thank for this authentic lemonade. This is a proper, old-fashioned lemonade cordial that has been allowed to steep so is deliciously lemony. If you're feeling particularly devil-may-care, add some limes. Mix it up. Live a little.

Mix the cordial with sparkly water for fizzy lemonade, or tap water for flat. It is delicious served with fresh mint sprigs and/or neat vodka, although that's maybe not one for the under-18s. It also freezes well into delicious ice lollies.

This recipe is suitable for bigger children to make (those that can be trusted around sharp knives and boiling water).

1. Grate the zest of the lemons (or lemons and limes) into a big heatproof bowl. Remove the remaining pith (white stuff) with a sharp knife and put it in the bin. It is bitter and not very nice. Pretend you still work in a pub while you slice the lemons (or lemons and limes) thinly and add them to the bowl of zest with their juice, pips, the lot.

2. Add the sugar and 1.7 litres of boiling water to the bowl. Stir gently until all the sugar has dissolved.

3. Cover with a clean tea towel and leave (preferably overnight) to cool.

4. Dissolve the citric acid in about 150ml of water and add to the lemonade; this gives it back the tartness the sugar has overpowered. Stir again.

5. Strain the lemonade through a nylon sieve, then funnel into a clean, empty two-litre bottle. Store in the fridge and use up within a week, diluted with still or fizzy water. Serve with sprigs of mint, frozen raspberries and ice. And straws.

Pudding

Top ten!

- **A very nice rice pudding**
- **Three-minute sponge**
- **Bread and butter pudding**
- **Double-baked apple and blackberry crumble**
- **Frozen rhubarb and custard**
- **Pear and ginger upside-down pudding**
- **Summer berry jelly**
- **Strawberry sauce**
- **Chocolate bombe**
- **Chocolate mousse for greedy goose**

Pudding. Dessert. Afters. Whatever you call it, wherever you are, if you are anything like us, you'll agree it is the very best part of a meal. Mumsnetters love a good pudding. And there are times when a bowl of yogurt or a piece of fruit – although virtuous – simply won't do. No, sometimes we want our bellies full to the brim so we can't move from the table, let alone waddle over to do the washing up.

We don't have a proper pudding every day. Much as we'd like to. Instead we save them for play dates, rainy days and weekend treats. Our favourite Monday night tradition is a bowl of soup, followed by leftover crumble from Sunday lunch. Virtue followed by decadence.

Dessert needn't be fancy. Cubes of Cheddar cheese drizzled with runny honey; Greek yogurt with pistachios; chopped fruit (children seem to find fruit less daunting if it is chopped up); or a whole bar of butterscotch chocolate. But sometimes we hanker after something more constructed. Like our Bread and butter pudding. Although, for trading standards purposes, we must warn you it is made neither with bread nor butter, but with croissants and a joyous, quivering custard that has our mouths watering just thinking about it. Believe us, it tastes as deliciously decadent as it sounds and must be eaten alone in full make-up and a little black dress. Possibly whilst reclining on a chaise longue.

You may want to keep the lipstick and black dress on when you're serving up the Chocolate bombe. It's the only way anyone will pay you any attention. The bombe is made from two ingredients close to a child's heart: ice cream and chocolate. Stick a sparkler in it and you will literally blow their minds.

A very nice rice pudding is reason enough to become a parent. It's a wonderful nursery pudding – creamy and sweet – but it's unlikely that you'd make it for yourself as a fully functioning adult. However, if you serve such a calcium-rich pud (it's full of double cream) to your child (and obviously have a large portion yourself) then you are a *great* parent. Suddenly you begin to see an unexpected upside to having kids.

You may, or may not, thank us for the recipe for Three-minute sponge. It is so utterly delicious you will want to eat it every day. It is also the perfect bribe with which to threaten your children. If we had a pound for the number of times we have said, 'If you don't eat your greens, there'll be no sponge pudding,' we would be on our way to Bermuda right now. In our private jet. Parenting experts would have a field day about using food as a threat, but hey, no-one's perfect...

On the healthier side (slightly) is Frozen rhubarb and custard, a combination made in heaven. Or our scrumptious Strawberry sauce which is perfectly lovely eaten (OK, drunk) on its own, but very tasty with brownies, shortbread, meringues, ice cream... In fact, the only limit is your imagination. And maybe your waistband.

A very nice rice pudding

Serves 4 adults

100g short-grain
  pudding rice
284ml pot of double
  cream, plus more
  to serve (optional)
750ml whole milk,
  plus more if needed, plus
  more to serve (optional)
120g sugar; whatever
  you've got in your
  cupboard is fine
1 vanilla pod
Jam, to serve (optional)

❦ Vegetarian

❊ Freezable

This is the water-into-wine miracle of the pudding world. Add a paltry amount of grain to far too much milk and expose it to gentle heat for a long time. Suddenly, something which looks like a culinary mistake miraculously turns into the most delectable pudding ever. This is a creamy, vanilla-y take on a classic and you have two choices about how to cook it, oven or hob, depending on how your day is panning out.

This recipe calls for a vanilla pod, more intense in flavour than vanilla extract. Vanilla pods are the seed containers of a climbing orchid. They are hand-pollinated and sun-dried and this labour-intensive process is reflected in the price. But treat them well and your vanilla pods will keep on giving. They will last up to two years in a dark, airtight container and, once you do decide to break them out, a pod can have more than one use. Once you've fished the pod from the rice pudding, give it a thorough rinse and let it dry out over a couple of days. Then stick it in a jar of sugar and in two weeks you'll have beautifully fragrant vanilla sugar, which can be stirred into porridge, sprinkled on pancakes or baked into a cake.

1. Put the rice, cream, milk and sugar into a large saucepan which has a lid, if you want to make it on the hob (which takes about an hour). If you'd rather make it in the oven (which takes about two hours and requires less stirring and checking), put them all into an ovenproof dish with a lid.

2. Split the vanilla pod lengthways and scrape the seeds into the rice pudding. Stick the empty pod in, too.

3. To cook on the hob: Put the lid on the saucepan and place it over a low heat. Bring to a gentle boil, then reduce the heat and simmer for 50–60 minutes, stirring now and then to stop it sticking. Once it's cooked (try a bit) it will look phenomenally milky. Like you've made a big mistake with the quantities. Trust us. As it cools the rice continues to absorb the milk and, once it's cool enough to eat, it will be perfect. Unless you have no willpower and an asbestos mouth, in which case it will still be too milky.

To oven cook: Preheat the oven to 170°C/fan 150°C/gas mark 3½. Cook the rice pudding for two hours. The oven dish takes more milk than cooking on the hob, but this is easier to adjust after the pudding has cooked rather than before. Just add some sploshes and stir in until you get the consistency you want.

4. Fish out the vanilla pod and serve, with a dash of cold milk, or jam, or cream (or both) to cool it down quickly for impatient little ones.

Three-minute sponge

Serves 4 adults

50g unsalted butter,
  well softened
50g caster sugar
1 egg, lightly beaten
2 tbsp milk
50g self-raising flour
2 tbsp golden syrup, or jam
Custard, to serve
  (not optional)

 Vegetarian

A lethal recipe to have up your sleeve, this has a golden syrup crown sitting atop a feathery light sponge. Delicious with custard. Steamed pudding is a wonderful British tradition and this one is brought bang up-to-date by the fact that it takes three minutes flat to cook in the microwave. Your taste buds will thank us, but your bathroom scales may not.

1. Cream together the butter and sugar until smooth. Mix in the egg and milk gradually, then gently fold in the flour.

2. Put the golden syrup or jam in the bottom of a microwave-safe bowl. Pour in the sponge mixture.

3. Cover and cook for three minutes on full power (for a 1,000 watt oven; if your microwave is weaker, up the cooking time). Take care, both the bowl and pudding will be hot, hot, hot.

4. Eat with custard. That is an order.

Bread and butter pudding

Serves 4 greedy adults

Unsalted butter, for
  greasing the dish
5 croissants
Raspberry jam (or any
  flavour that takes
  your fancy)
50g sultanas
200ml milk
200ml double cream
1 tsp vanilla extract
3 eggs, lightly beaten
75g caster sugar

☛ **You will need**
20 x 18cm baking dish.

❦ **Vegetarian**

Words cannot describe how gorgeous this pudding is, and its rather prosaic name does not do it justice. The 'bread' is actually croissants layered with raspberry jam, studded with sultanas and steeped in a vanilla custard. You could cook it for someone you love, or – our preferred option - eat it in bed on your own. It's also a good (though indulgent) way to use up day-old croissants.

1. Butter a 20 x 18cm baking dish.

2. Slice the croissants in half horizontally so they split completely apart and spread one side with jam.

3. Layer the jammy croissant halves on the bottom of the dish, jam-side up, then sprinkle over the sultanas. Layer the remaining croissant halves on top, cut-side down.

4. In a saucepan, heat the milk, cream and vanilla extract until very hot but *not* boiling. Remove from the heat and leave to cool slightly.

5. Put the eggs and sugar in a bowl and whisk with a balloon whisk or electric whisk until thick and well combined. This should take about three minutes. Gradually pour in the cooled milk mixture (if the mixture was very hot, the eggs would scramble), continuing to whisk until it is all mixed in. It should now resemble a thin custard.

6. Pour the custard over the croissants and press them down a little with your fingers to make sure they absorb it. Leave to stand for at least five and up to 30 minutes (don't skip this step, it allows your pud to absorb the custard in a dreamy way) while you preheat the oven to 180°C/fan 160°C/gas mark 4.

7. Half-fill a large roasting tray with warm water and carefully place the pudding dish in the centre. It is about to have a nice bath. Bake in the oven for 35–45 minutes, until the pudding is browned on top.

8. Stand the pudding for five minutes, then eat. Lick your lips.

Double-baked apple and blackberry crumble

Serves 4 adults

For the filling
2 Bramley apples
50g brown sugar
Juice of ½ lemon
200g blackberries

For the crumble
250g plain flour (or half
  plain and half wholemeal,
  if you prefer)
225g brown sugar
115g unsalted butter,
  chilled and cut into cubes

🌱 **Vegetarian**

❄ **Freezable**
The cooked fruit and the
crumble topping can be
frozen separately.

The NCT should run crumble-making courses alongside all that birth stuff. So you gave birth without an epidural, but who's going to remember that on a rainy Sunday afternoon when your child is seven? They will remember crumble, though. This is a good one to start with: simple, delicious and quick. As you get more confident you can adapt the filling to suit the season (plums and ginger?) and the crumble to suit your mood (nutty?).

Although easy, crumble can be a bit temperamental and that's because it likes it to be nice and chilly. Think pastry rather than cake. So the butter needs to be fridge-cold. When you are ready to use it, cut it up small. This means you can mix it into the flour more quickly with your fingertips, so it stays cold. If you have got hot hands, it's worth running them under cold water beforehand, to keep the temperature down.

1. Preheat the oven to 180°C/fan 160°C/gas mark 4.

2. Peel and core the apples, then chop them into small pieces roughly 1cm square (but don't get the measuring tape out).

3. Place the apples in an ovenproof dish, pour over the sugar and the lemon juice and toss so all the apple is coated. Pop in the oven for 15 minutes.

4. Meanwhile, make the crumble. Put the flour, sugar and chopped-up butter in a bowl. Rub together with your fingertips until the mixture resembles breadcrumbs. Don't over-mix; it doesn't matter if there are some lumps of butter or chunks of sugar, because that gives the crumble its rustic consistency.

5. Add the blackberries to the baking apples, then return the dish to the oven for another five minutes.

6. Pour the crumble mix over the top, so it's evenly distributed. Bake for a final 30 minutes, or until golden and crunchy.

Frozen rhubarb and custard

Serves 4 adults

2 x 500g pots of
  ready-made custard
600g jar of rhubarb
  compote, available from
  most large supermarkets
Ginger thins, to serve
  (optional but lovely)

 Vegetarian

✳ Freezable

Rhubarb and custard is such a heavenly combination. The way the sweetness of the creamy custard cuts through the tartness of the rhubarb has us more excited than is probably right and proper. We're a little bit in love.

This is not supposed to be a perfectly layered confection, more of a custardy/rhubarby swirl.

1. Custard freezes really well (it makes delicious lollies) and here all you do is take a shallow, freezerproof Tupperware container with a lid and simply layer the custard and compote. Start with three spoons of the custard, then two spoons of the compote, then carry on until finished, ideally ending with a layer of custard. Put the lid on the container and bung it in the freezer.

2. After a couple of hours the rhubarb and custard should be semi-frozen (this is when it is most delicious). If you've left it too long and it has frozen solid, remove from the freezer for 30 minutes before serving, to soften. Spoon it into bowls and – if you like – serve it with ginger thins.

Pear and ginger upside-down pudding

Serves 8 adults

125g unsalted butter, well softened, plus more for the tin
125g self-raising flour
1 tsp baking powder
1–2 tsp ground ginger
55g golden syrup
3 pears, peeled, cored and each cut into 8
125g soft brown sugar
2 eggs, lightly beaten
A little milk, if needed
Crème fraîche, or cream, to serve

☛ **You will need**
20cm round cake tin.

❦ **Vegetarian**

So easy, you could make this standing on your head. But then it wouldn't be an upside-down pudding, so where would we be? This slight twist on a classic is very easy to whip up and has an unchallenging ingredients list. Most people could conjure it up using stuff from their kitchen cupboard and the local corner shop.

1. Preheat the oven to 180°C/fan 160°C/gas mark 4. Butter a 20cm round cake tin and line the base with greaseproof paper. If your tin has a loose base, cut the greaseproof paper slightly too large, so it seals the edges and doesn't let the syrup escape.

2. Put the flour, baking powder and ginger into a small bowl and stir. Once they are well mixed, set aside.

3. Put the golden syrup into a small pan and gently heat until it becomes runny. Pour into the cake tin, then arrange the pears on top. It looks pretty if you put the thin ends of the pears at the centre of the tin and the thicker ends at the outside edge, a bit like petals on a daisy.

4. In a separate large bowl, cream the butter and sugar until light and airy. Add the eggs gradually, while continuing to beat.

5. Find that bowl of flour and gradually fold its contents into the batter using a spoon. Once everything is well mixed, the batter should drop off the end of the spoon in a big dollop. If it's too stiff, add some milk. It's important the consistency is right, otherwise the sponge won't coat the pears properly.

6. Pour the mixture over the pears and put in the oven for 40 minutes. If it starts to brown too much at the end, cover the top of the pudding with foil. When you take it out of the oven it should be well-risen, golden and spring back when you press it.

7. Leave the pudding in the tin for a few minutes before you turn it out on to a plate, pear-side upwards, removing the paper. Serve with crème fraîche, or cream if you're feeling decadent.

Summer berry jelly

Serves 4 adults

4 gelatine leaves
Elderflower cordial
150g berries, such
  as raspberries
  and strawberries

🌱 **Vegetarian**
For vegetarians, use
vegetarian gelatine from
large supermarkets (or agar
agar from health food shops)
and follow the instructions
on the package to set 570ml
of liquid.

Berries suspended in the pale glow of elderflower cordial are like summer in a glass. Don't be put off by the use of gelatine leaves, rather than a pack of jelly. It's just as easy and lets you play around with flavours more.

If it's not summer and berries are thin on the ground, adapt. In winter, squeeze a cocktail of clementine, satsuma and orange juices instead of using cordial. You can use pretty much any juice or fruit, whatever tickles your fancy, although remember some fruits such as pineapples and kiwis have an enzyme that prevents setting. Heating the juice through should destroy that enzyme.

If it's a birthday or special occasion, why not chuck in some sweetie snakes or gummy bears instead of the fruit?

1. Soak the gelatine leaves in cold water for five minutes.

2. Dilute the elderflower cordial with water according to the instructions on the bottle. You will need 570ml (one pint; we revert to old-fashioned measures when talking gelatine!) of liquid in total. Put it in a saucepan and heat until it simmers. Take off the heat and leave until just hand-hot.

3. Squeeze any excess water from the gelatine leaves and pop them in the saucepan. Let them dissolve, stirring occasionally, for two minutes.

4. Divide the elderflower jelly between four small containers; little glass tumblers look really pretty. Drop in a selection of berries; if using strawberries, cut them in halves or quarters. They will fall to different depths depending on their weight.

5. Pop the jellies in the fridge for a few hours to set. Eight hours is recommended but, since you are eating the jellies straight from their containers rather than emptying them from moulds, four hours should do it (though don't tempt fate if it's your first time making it; leave it for the longer period, especially if it's for guests).

Strawberry sauce

Makes a large cupful of sauce

300g strawberries
50g icing sugar
1 tsp lemon juice

To make 1 sundae
Handful of mixed berries
Scoop of vanilla ice cream
1 meringue (optional)
Whipped cream
Sprigs of mint (optional)

❦ Vegetarian

This is a recipe for a proper strawberry sauce. Not that stuff with an alarmingly long ingredients list that comes out of a squeezy bottle at the ice cream van. It is great with brownies, folded through whipped cream, with ice-cream sundaes, meringues and shortbread. You get the picture. It is also a great way to use up past-their-best strawberries.

1. Wash the strawberries and hull them. Pop in a blender or food processor and whizz up with the icing sugar and lemon juice.

2. If you want a smooth sauce, push it through a nylon sieve.

To make a fruit sundae

Take a tall glass and layer any summer berries you have to hand – strawberries, blueberries, raspberries – with a good dollop of vanilla ice cream in between each layer of fruit. If you have any meringue, crumble that in as well. Top it all with some whipped cream, then drizzle the strawberry sauce generously all over it. Add some sprigs of mint, if you're feeling fancy.

Chocolate bombe

Serves 8 adults

100g good-quality
  dark chocolate
2 eggs, separated
4 tsp caster sugar
240ml double cream
½ tsp vanilla extract
100g (half a packet) of
  sponge fingers (or enough
  to line the top and sides
  of your chosen container)
150ml whipping cream
1 tbsp icing sugar
Chocolate shavings,
  to decorate

☛ **You will need**
A freezerproof dish: a silicone
dish or a deep cake tin will
both work well.

❦ **Vegetarian**

✳ **Freezable**

Put some lipstick on, you've got competition. Walking into a room with this baby will create a silence. Jaws will drop. You will go largely unnoticed. This is a dream of a pudding, a cloud-like confection of chocolate and cream. Make it once and kids will request it again and again. Once you've dropped the Bombe, there's no going back.

In an ideal world this would be the perfect recipe to make the day before. However, freezers have a tendency to be really *really* cold, so it could end up rock solid. The best way is to make it a few hours before you serve it. Or take it out about 30 minutes ahead of serving. Or just slice it very thinly. Any which way, it's delicious.

1. Melt the chocolate in a bain-marie or the microwave (see page 256) and set aside to cool. In a separate bowl, mix together the egg yolks and caster sugar with a balloon whisk.

2. In a saucepan, heat one-third (80ml) of the double cream until it steams. Add half of it to the egg mixture, stirring constantly. Return the warm egg blend to the other half of the hot cream in the saucepan and cook over a low heat, stirring constantly for a few more minutes. Remove from the heat and stir in the vanilla and cooled chocolate. Cover the bowl.

3. Chill this chocolate custard mixture for one hour; don't let it set hard.

Later...
4. Using an electric whisk, beat the remaining 160ml of double cream in a separate bowl to stiff peaks. Stir a couple of tablespoons of it into the chocolate custard, then gently fold in the rest using a spoon.

5. Line a freezerproof dish with foil, then arrange the sponge fingers on the base and up the sides. Spoon the chocolate mixture into the dish, cover with foil and place in the freezer for a couple of hours, until set.

Later still...
6. Whip the whipping cream, then whip in the icing sugar. In a separate bowl, whip the egg whites to stiff peaks. Gently fold into the cream.

7. Take the pudding out of the freezer, turn it on to a plate and remove the foil. Cover with the cream mixture. Sprinkle chocolate shavings all over and return to the freezer for 30 minutes, or until you serve.

Chocolate mousse for greedy goose

Makes 4 small mousses

75g milk chocolate,
   chopped or broken up
2 eggs, separated
25g unsalted butter, melted
2 tbsp caster sugar
Gingernut biscuits,
   chocolate curls, halved
   strawberries, and/or
   cocoa powder, to serve

❤ Vegetarian

✳ Freezable

This pudding is named after the children's book by Julia Donaldson. As it uses milk chocolate instead of plain, it is not overwhelmingly rich, making it perfect for the whole family. It is light and fluffy and oh, so chocolatey. Easy to make, too. The eggs in this are not cooked, so the usual caveats apply (don't serve it to pregnant women, very young children, or those with weakened immune systems).

1. Melt the chocolate in a bain-marie or the microwave (see page 256).

2. Wait a couple of minutes for the chocolate to cool slightly, then mix it with the egg yolks and butter, stirring all the time so the eggs don't cook.

3. Whisk the egg whites lightly, then gradually whisk in the sugar until the mixture is shiny and stiff.

4. Fold the two mixtures together. Divide between four small glasses or espresso cups and chill until set.

5. Eat. Good with gingernut biscuits dipped in, or chocolate curls on the top, or halved strawberries on the side, or dusted with cocoa powder. Or all the above.

Baking

Top ten!

- **Everyday lemon drizzle cake**
- **Apple cakejack**
- **Standing-on-your-head banana bread**
- **Victorious sponge**
- **The world's easiest fairy cakes**
- **Teenage mutant ginger turtles**
- **Chocolate bribe biscuits**
- **Chocolate, cranberry and hazelnut flapjacks**
- **Guaranteed-super-squidgy chocolate brownies**
- **Chocolate, almond and chestnut cake**

There's something magical about baking. It's not just the treat you get at the end of it, although that definitely helps. It's the process. The cracking, the pouring, the beating, the licking (an integral part), then the sweet smell that wafts out of the kitchen door and says, 'This is a home'.

Because cakes can do that. A home-baked cake can make you feel happy, cared for, loved. A beautifully constructed birthday cake may cost your sanity, but your child will remember it and the feeling it gave them for the rest of their life.

Your memories of baking the cake may be quite different. The feeling you had as it collapsed on contact with the cold air, how you felt when the icing slowly slid off the sides and how, as a bedraggled heap on the floor, you contemplated the 20 party bags still to be filled before morning...

The secret to a good cake is not to bake wildly. Baking is a science and recipes are best followed to the letter. Don't bake a different cake every time; get to know a recipe, perfect it, make it your friend. Soon you'll be able to do it in your sleep, and knocking up banana bread for the school cake sale, or for when a friend's had a baby, will be a cost-effective and easy way of saying you care.

Baking the same cake each time also means that you won't get to the end of the recipe and realise that you don't have the right-sized cake tin (the recipe calls for a 20cm cake tin, but you only have a 25cm? Scale up the ingredients by 1.5 and increase the cooking time). Or that you need room temperature butter but yours is still in the fridge (damn that fridge-cold butter! Here's a top tip: fill a small bowl with hot tap water. Stick half a pat of butter in it for five seconds and then retrieve. It should be perfect).

It might also mean you've invested in the correctly sized silicone cake mould – ah, silicone, the lazy cook's answer to everything – so you don't need to butter and line the tin. If you do have a tin rather than silicone, remember to line it properly. The best way is to draw around the base on to greaseproof paper and then cut. We then usually take a small wodge of butter and smear around the sides and base of the tin so the greaseproof paper sticks to it.

The cakes that are in this chapter will see you through the challenges of parenting. Low-energy afternoons, in desperate need of a pick-me-up? The Everyday lemon drizzle cake takes minutes to throw together. Wet weekend? Get them cutting out Teenage mutant ginger turtles (try to ignore the worryingly clean fingernails at the end of it). Afternoon tea, or you just want to impress the in-laws? The Victorious sponge will have them begging for more.

We're not the first ones to have rumbled the power of cake. Generations of women have baked for their children, as our mums baked for us, and it's that repetition and continuity that makes it special.

That's the best thing about baking – it transforms. The alchemy of dry heat on eggs, sugar, flour and fat is something that never ceases to amaze. And the transformation isn't restricted to the cake. It transforms us. We may have had the day from hell and a kitchen floor that hasn't been washed for weeks, but stick a home-made cake in our hands and suddenly we're the parent of our dreams, serene in a floral apron. Everything is in control! Nobody panic! We've got cake!

So mix up those ingredients and put them in the oven. Twenty minutes later, stick the kettle on. Cut yourself a slice of cake. You're home.

Everyday lemon drizzle cake

Makes 8 adult slices

For the cake
175g unsalted butter,
  well softened, plus
  more to butter the tin
175g caster sugar
170g self-raising flour
2 eggs, lightly beaten
1½ tsp baking powder
3 tbsp milk
Finely grated zest of
  1 unwaxed lemon

For the syrup
Juice of the zested lemon
60g caster sugar

☛ **You will need**
20cm round cake tin.

❦ **Vegetarian**

✳ **Freezable**

By calling this an 'everyday' cake we do not mean that it's a humble offering. Oh no. We mean it's so easy to knock together that a sugary-lemony hit is possible every day. Yes, this recipe is good news. With ingredients even the slackest parent will find in their cupboard, all you need is ten minutes to whizz it all together. Oh, and an oven.

1. Preheat the oven to 180°C/fan 160°C/gas mark 4. Lightly butter a 20cm round cake tin and line the base with greaseproof paper.

2. Put all the cake ingredients in a large bowl and beat with a hand-held electric whisk until they are fully mixed and a pale yellow colour. Pour into the prepared cake tin and bake for 35–40 minutes, or until the top bounces back when you press it lightly, or a knife or skewer comes out clean from the centre of the cake.

3. Leave the cake in the tin and immediately heat the zested lemon in the microwave, if you have one, for 10 seconds (it makes it easier to juice). Let it cool a little, then juice it. Place the juice in a bowl and stir in the caster sugar. Use a fork to prick the cake all over while it is still hot from the oven, then drizzle the lemon syrup over the top of the cake.

4. Once the cake has completely cooled, remove it from the cake tin, lemon syrup-side up, peel off the paper and serve.

Apple cakejack

Makes 9–12 slices

200g unsalted butter,
  plus more to butter the tin
200g soft brown sugar
140g self-raising flour
170g porridge oats
3 tsp ground cinnamon
1½ apples (or pears), cored
  and thinly sliced, about
  16 slices per apple

☛ **You will need**
20cm square tray-bake tin or
small roasting tin for flapjacks
or
20 x 10cm loaf tin for a cake.

❦ **Vegetarian**

✳ **Freezable**

♥ **The health bit**
If you make cakes or biscuits
at home rather than buying
them, you have complete
control of what goes in them.
Mwah-hah-hah! This means
more fruit and less sugar,
if you are so inclined.

Made from oats, apples and flour, it's difficult to decide exactly where this recipe falls on the cake–flapjack continuum. Bake it in a loaf tin and you get a cake, spread it more thinly in a tray-bake tin and you get flapjacks.

1. Preheat your oven to 190°C/fan 170°C/gas mark 5. Then lightly butter the base and sides of a 20cm square tray-bake tin if you want a flapjack, or a 20 x 10cm loaf tin for a more cakey bake. Line the base of your chosen tin with greaseproof paper.

2. Place the butter and sugar in a large saucepan over a low heat and stir until the butter melts. Take off the heat and stir in the flour, oats and cinnamon. Mix well. Spoon half the mixture into the tin and place the sliced apples or pears on top. Cover these with the rest of the oat mixture. Bake in the oven for 25–30 minutes.

3. Once they are cooked, let the cakejacks cool in their tin slightly. If you have made them in a thinner flapjack style, cut into fingers or squares while they are warm, then leave them to cool and harden in their tin. If you are using a loaf tin, treat it as you would a cake: wait for it to cool a little, then turn out on a wire rack, peel off the paper and let it cool completely before you slice it.

Standing-on-your-head banana bread

Makes 1 loaf

110g unsalted butter, well
  softened, plus more
  to butter the tin
2 big bananas,
  the riper the better
170g caster sugar
2 eggs, lightly beaten
225g self-raising flour

☞ **You will need**
900g loaf tin.

♥ **Vegetarian**

❄ **Freezable**

♥ **The health bit**
Bananas add sweetness
to cakes, meaning you
don't need to add as much
sugar. This could mean less
bouncing off walls. But don't
hold us to that.

This is so-called because it is the world's easiest banana bread. It is so simple you could bake it standing on your head whilst ironing/Googling obscure 1980s pop lyrics/posting on Mumsnet (delete as applicable). It rises beautifully and looks worthy of 'best in show' at the Women's Institute.

Banana bread makes a brilliant breakfast or after-school snack, and is a great way of using up any blackening bananas festering in the fruit bowl. It is easy, quick, cheap and counts towards your five-a-day.

1. Preheat the oven to 200°C/fan 180°C/gas mark 6 and butter a 900g loaf tin.

2. Mash the bananas with a fork.

3. Cream the butter and sugar together until light and fluffy. Beat in the eggs. Add the squashed bananas and stir in the flour. (Don't bother sifting.)

4. Pour the mixture into the tin and bake for about 50 minutes, until well-risen and golden brown.

5. Let it cool slightly in the tin before transferring to a wire rack. Or scoffing the lot.

Victorious sponge

Serves 8 greedy adults

For the cake

175g-ish unsalted butter,
 well softened, plus more
 to butter the tins
3 eggs, lightly beaten
175g-ish caster sugar
175g-ish self-raising flour

For the filling

150ml double cream
Handful of raspberries
Icing sugar, to taste,
 plus more to dust

☛ **You will need**

2 x 20cm round cake tins.

❦ **Vegetarian**

❄ **Freezable**

Of course baking isn't something you should be competitive about. However, if you could knock something up that blows everyone else out of the water (*and* is really easy, but no one need know that), wouldn't you do it? With just four ingredients and a flamboyant filling, this is that cake. Serve it on your best plate and use a doily to really up the ante. Bake it for the school cake sale, a family gathering, birthday party or just a decadent afternoon tea and feel a wave of smugness wash over you.

1. Preheat the oven to 180°C/fan 160°C/gas mark 4. Lightly butter two 20cm round cake tins and line the bases with greaseproof paper.

2. Weigh the eggs in their shells and use this weight to determine how much butter, sugar and flour to use. So, if three eggs weigh 175g, then you need 175g each of butter, sugar and flour.

3. Using an electric whisk, cream the sugar and butter together until they turn pale yellow. Then beat in the eggs, a little at a time, to prevent the mixture from curdling. If it does, add a spoonful of flour and stir it in.

4. Then sift the remaining flour into the mix and fold it in. Once it is fully incorporated (don't overwork it or it won't be as fluffy), divide the batter between the tins. Place in the oven and bake for 20–25 minutes.

5. When the cakes are well risen and spring back to the touch, or a skewer comes out clean, remove them from the oven. Leave to cool in the tins for 10 minutes, then cover a wire rack with a folded tea towel to prevent marks and turn out the cakes on to them. Peel off the papers and leave to cool completely before attempting to add the filling (or it will just melt).

6. To prepare the filling, whip the double cream until it billows. Stir the raspberries in with a fork, crushing them up so they make the cream a pretty pink colour. Taste and, if needed, add a touch of icing sugar.

7. Put a doily on a plate and place the least-attractive looking cake on the doily. Spread it with a thick layer of the filling, then place the other sponge carefully on top, baked crust uppermost. Add a dusting of icing sugar, stand back and admire.

The world's easiest fairy cakes

Makes 12 cakes

125g self-raising flour
125g unsalted butter,
   well softened
125g caster sugar
1 tsp baking powder
1 tsp vanilla extract
2 eggs, lightly beaten
1 tbsp milk

☛ You will need
Fairy cake tray; 12 fairy
cake cases.

❦ Vegetarian

❄ Freezable
The cooked, cooled cakes
are freezable before icing.

Hands over ears please, devout bakers. The following admission may shock. In the past we have bought supermarket fairy cakes and pretended we baked them ourselves. But since discovering this recipe, those days are gone. In the time it takes to walk to the shops, you can rustle up these beauties instead.

If you would like chocolate fairy cakes, substitute 40g of the flour with the same weight of cocoa powder. Both kinds are best eaten whole, when your children aren't looking.

1. Preheat the oven to 200°C/fan 180°C/gas mark 6 and line a fairy cake tray with fairy cake cases.

2. Put all the ingredients except the milk in a food processor, or blitz in a bowl with an electric whisk, until smooth. Add the milk, blitz again, then spoon into the cake cases.

3. Cook for 15 minutes, until the cakes have risen and are golden. Stick a skewer through the largest one and check it comes out clean. If it does, the cakes are ready. Leave them to cool on a wire rack before icing (see pages 256–259), or sticking in your mouth whole.

Teenage mutant ginger turtles

Makes 20 large turtles

350g plain flour,
  plus more to dust
1 tsp bicarbonate of soda
2 tsp ground ginger
125g unsalted butter,
  cubed and chilled
175g brown sugar
1 egg
2 tsp golden syrup
Glacé icing (see page 258),
  to decorate (optional)

☞ **You will need**
Turtle-shaped cutters, or any
other fun cutters.

♥ **Vegetarian**

❄ **Freezable**
The dough can be frozen
before cooking.

Does the yoke of patriarchy weigh heavy on your shoulders?
If so, throw gingerbread men into the cooling oven of history
and upgrade your cookie cutters. This delicious recipe and an
ever-changing cast of cutters means hours of fun on every
occasion. Wet February half-terms can be brightened up with
Valentine hearts and Hallowe'en can be filled with spooky skulls.
Who knew patriarchy was such a flimsy construct?

1. Preheat the oven to 160°C/fan 140°C/gas mark 3. Line two large baking
trays with greaseproof paper.

2. Sift the flour, bicarbonate of soda and ginger into a mixing bowl.
Then, using your fingers, rub the butter into the dry ingredients until
the mixture resembles breadcrumbs. Stir in the sugar.

3. Break the egg into a separate bowl or cup and add the golden syrup
to it. Stir. Make a well in the flour mix, pour the egg mixture into it and
give it all a good stir.

4. At this point you'll be faced with a bowl of brown-coloured crumb
mixture and you'll be wondering how that ever becomes a dough. Take
a handful of the mix in one hand and, using the other hand, squish and
knead it together until the colour becomes uniform and the texture
smooth. This is when it is ready to roll out. If your kitchen (or hands)
are too hot the dough may become gloopy, so put it in the fridge for
a few minutes to firm up.

5. Flour a work surface and a rolling pin with plain flour and roll the
dough to about 3mm thick, then use the cutters to cut out shapes.

6. Place the cookies on the prepared baking trays with a little room to
spread and put in the oven for 12–15 minutes. When they are golden,
remove from the oven and transfer to a wire rack to cool (a palette knife
is good for this). Decorate with glacé icing, if you like.

Chocolate bribe biscuits

Makes 15

100g caster sugar

50g unsalted butter,
  well softened

4 tbsp Greek yogurt

100g plain flour,
  plus more to dust

25g cocoa powder

1 tsp vanilla extract

40g bag of chocolate
  buttons or chips

❤ **Vegetarian**

❄ **Freezable**
The biscuits can be frozen
before cooking.

It's raining. The kids are looking mutinous. Can it get any worse? Oh no... the TV's just broken! Never fear, chocolate bribe biscuits are here. These little beauties, crammed with chocolate buttons, will make any situation better. You could use posh chocolate for the chocolate chips, but, for us, chocolate buttons win every time. Get the kids to help you make them and you've got 30 minutes of happy families with gooey chocolate biscuits to bribe them with at the end. Result.

1. Preheat the oven to 180°C/fan 160°C/gas mark 4. Line a large baking tray with greaseproof paper.

2. Mix the sugar, butter and yogurt with an electric whisk until light and fluffy.

3. Sift the flour and cocoa powder into the mixture, then lightly fold them in using a spoon. Add the vanilla extract and chocolate buttons or chips, and continue mixing until you have a dough.

4. Flour your hands and divide the dough into 15 equal pieces. Roll each piece into a ball and place on the tray in neat, well-spaced lines.

5. Take a fork and wet it in a cup of water. Press the tines into the centre of a dough ball and push to flatten the ball. Then, wet the fork again and press at right angles to the first pattern to form a criss-cross on top of each biscuit. Or just press each biscuit twice in parallel, as in the photo. The chocolate buttons might make the biscuits a little snaggly, but that just adds to their charm!

6. Bake the biscuits for 15 minutes, then remove from the oven. Let cool slightly, then transfer the biscuits to a wire rack (a palette knife is good for this) to cool completely.

Chocolate, cranberry and hazelnut flapjacks

Makes 8, depending on portion control

150g unsalted butter
4 tbsp golden syrup
215g porridge oats
100g hazelnuts,
  chopped in half
130g dried cranberries
80g dark or milk
  chocolate, broken
  into small chunks

☛ **You will need**
20 x 10cm tray-bake tin,
or small roasting tin.

❦ **Vegetarian**

❄ **Freezable**

This flapjack is for the seriously sweet-toothed. It is lethally good. But there is a credit:debit equation to be made. Credit: slow-release energy of the porridge oats, then the cranberries and nuts. Debit: golden syrup and not insignificant amounts of chocolate. You do the maths.

1. Preheat the oven to 190°C/fan 170°C/gas mark 5. Line a 20 x 10cm tray-bake tin with greaseproof paper.

2. In a large saucepan heat the butter and syrup – careful, this is hot – over a low heat until everything has melted. Give it a good stir and add everything else except the chocolate. Give it another good stir. Try not to nibble. Last, but by no means least, add the chocolate and give it a quick stir. It will start to melt and marble through the mixture. Yum.

3. Pour the mixture into the tin and push it firmly down. (If there are air pockets, the finished flapjacks will crumble when you cut into them.)

4. Bake in the oven for 20 minutes, or until firm to the touch; it should be slightly tinged with brown around the edges. Now look to your willpower: you *must* leave it to cool completely before taking it out of the tin, peeling off the paper and cutting it. This is hard as it is *so* delicious. Definitely one of our favourites.

Guaranteed-super-squidgy chocolate brownies

Makes 12 large or 24 small, depending on how sweet your tooth

200g unsalted butter, plus more to butter the tin
200g dark chocolate (70% cocoa solids), roughly chopped
3 eggs, lightly beaten
½ tsp vanilla extract
250g caster sugar
115g plain flour
Pinch of salt
50g milk or white chocolate, chopped
50g hazelnuts, chopped (optional)

☛ **You will need**
20 x 30cm brownie or tray-bake tin, or small roasting tin.

♥ **Vegetarian**

✱ **Freezable**

These are the best brownies in the world. The trick is not to over-cook them, so they're still squidgy inside. They are quite flat, which makes them the perfect size to slip in your handbag or buggy for crafty chocolatey emergencies. Your emergencies, not the kids', naturally.

1. Preheat the oven to 200°C/fan 180°C/gas mark 6. Find a 20 x 30cm brownie or tray-bake tin (or a similar-sized small roasting tin), butter it and line the base with greaseproof paper.

2. In a saucepan, melt the butter and dark chocolate together. Take it off the heat, then simply add all the other ingredients apart from the milk or white chocolate and nuts – if you're using them – and mix well.

3. Pour into the tin, then scatter the milk or white chocolate and the nuts evenly over the surface, poking them down a little to stop them burning.

4. Bake for 20 minutes. By this time, the top surface of the brownies should have started to crack but the insides will still be soft and gooey. If you overcook them, they'll still be delicious, but a little more cakey and a bit less squidgy.

5. Leave the brownies to go completely cold in the tin before peeling off the paper and cutting them into squares.

Chocolate, almond and chestnut cake

Serves 8–12 adults

190g unsalted butter, well
    softened, plus more
    to butter the tin
500ml milk
200g pack of vacuum-
    packed, peeled and
    cooked chestnuts
180g caster sugar
5 eggs, separated
180g ground almonds
200g dark chocolate
    (70% cocoa solids),
    chopped into small pieces

To serve
Icing sugar, to dust
Berries, cherries and/or
    cream or Greek yogurt

☛ **You will need**
20cm round cake tin,
about 10cm deep.

❧ **Vegetarian**

❋ **Freezable**

This is a cake to fall in love with. Dense and chocolatey, ground almonds and chestnuts are used instead of flour, making it perfect for the wheat-free cake lover.

It is best eaten straight from the oven so all the chocolate chips are still gooey, but it's still yummy when eaten cold for elevenses (OK, breakfast) the next day.

Although there are a few stages to this cake, all of them are very simple, making it practically foolproof. Honest.

1. Preheat the oven to 180°C/fan 160°C/gas mark 4. Butter a 20cm round cake tin (choose one that is about 10cm deep) and line the base with greaseproof paper.

2. Put the milk in a small saucepan, add the chestnuts and let them simmer for five minutes until they have softened. Don't sigh. This is the most fiddly bit. Remove the chestnuts from the milk and chop into smallish pieces. (Discard the milk.)

3. Using an electric whisk or food mixer, beat the butter with 140g of the caster sugar until the mixture is pale and fluffy. Add the egg yolks one at a time, mixing well. Next, using a spoon, stir in the ground almonds, chopped chocolate and chestnuts.

4. In a large bowl, whisk the egg whites until foamy. Add the remaining 40g sugar and whisk until firm and glossy. Using a spoon, carefully fold the egg whites into the cake batter, then pour into the prepared tin.

5. Bake for 50 minutes until the cake is firm to the touch and a skewer comes out clean. Leave it in the tin for 10 minutes, then turn out on to a wire rack, baked-side up. Peel off the paper. You can either allow the cake to cool or serve it warm. Dust it with icing sugar. Eat on its own, or with berries, a dollop of cream or Greek yogurt. Yum.

Acknowledgements

First and foremost we at Mumsnet owe a huge debt of gratitude to all the Mumsnetters who helped us so much with this project. From those who contributed the recipes in the first place, to the recipe testers who helped us whittle down an initial cast of hundreds of recipes to the final 120 you find in these pages, we simply wouldn't have been able to write this book without them.

We also wouldn't be here without having had the great good luck to find our authors – sisters, bloggers and mums Claire and Lucy McDonald – who were instantaneously on our wavelength.

At Bloomsbury the editorial team of Natalie Hunt, Xa Shaw Stewart and Alison Glossop expertly steered the project from concept to the book you're holding in your hands today, while Marina Asenjo is responsible for how beautifully printed it is. We would also like to thank Myfanwy Vernon-Hunt for coming up with the design, and Lucy Bannell for her editing. Thanks, too, to our agent Will Francis.

Photographer Jill Mead took the gorgeous pictures, ably supported by Polly Webb-Wilson and Bianca Nice, who managed the brilliant styling of props and food.

And the nutritionist Fiona Hunter was instrumental in providing a healthy insight to the final recipes that were picked.

The full list of Mumsnetter recipe testers
3rdnparty, 41notTrendy, addictedisback, AgentProvocateur, Aimingtobeaperfectionist, alarkaspree, Ally1968, arfur, Arion, armedtotheteeth, ArthurShappey, Asmywhimsytakesme, AWomanCalledHorse, BadBuddha, BadRoly, Bakingnovice, ballstoit, BarmeeMarmee, barraboy, Barristermum, beanandspud, BellaOfTheBalls, BetterTogether, BigFlipFlop, birdyarms, Biscuitsandtea, Blatherskite, blondieminx, bluebump, BlueEyeshadow, BlueyDragon, bulletwithbutterflywings, CachuHwch, CagneyNLacey, cairnterrier, CakeExpectations, californiaburrito, CamperFan, CandiceMariePratt, CaseyShraeger, cashmere, catinboots, Catsmamma, catwithflowers, champagnesupernova, Chaosandcupcakes, ChaosTrulyReigns, CheeryCherry, Chepstowmonkey, CherryBlossom27, chinley, chocolateistheenemy, chutestoonarrow, claimedbyme, Cluelessnchaos, clumber, cmotdibbler, Cocoacloset, cocoplops, ComeAlongPond, Commotionintheocean, Continentalkat, ControlGeek, Coops79, countingdown, CrystalTits, danytargaryen, DameMargotFountain, Dazzlingdeborahrose, debka, Deemented, DeepPurple, Denise77, DharmaBumpkin, DialMforMummy, Dimdommilpot, dickyduckydido, DilysPrice,

Doilooklikeatourist, dontmixthecolours, DorsetKnob, Drcrab, DreamsTurnToGoldDust, DrHamstertoyou, droitwichmummy, DuchessOFAvon, DustyMoth, DustyOwl, Dysgu, elderflowergranita, Elkieb, esmeweatherwax, EstherRancid, eyestightshut, fallenempires, Faverolles, Fedupnagging, feetheart, FIFBEBE, Fillybuster, firawla, Firewall, Fivegomadindorset, Fivesacrowd, fluffacloud, FolkGirl, FortiesCromarty, Franke, FrankWippery, Frontpaw, Frootshoots, FruitSaladIsNotPudding, Gazzalw, geogteach, Geordieminx, Glitterfairys, goatshavestrangeeyes, Goldface, goplayout, GrandPoohBah, GreatGooglyMoogly, grumpydwarf, GwendolineMaryLacey, GwennieF, habbibu, HairyPotter, Halfling, halfmumhalfbiscuit, HappySunflower, higgsbosom, highlandbird, Hugandroll, ibbydibby, ICanTuckMyBoobsInMyPockets, ICutMyFootOnOccamsRazor, ILikeToMoveItMoveIt, Imnotcute, intravenouscoffee, Irishmammybread, ItsNotUnusualToBe, IWantAChipButty, JammySplodger, Janx, Jcee, jemw, jennycrofter, Jobnockey, johnworf, JulesJules, Justblameitonthecuervodude, Karate, kimmi, karoleann, Kdiddy, Kelbells, KindleAddict, Kittenkatzen, Kittycatcat, KnockKnockPenny, KurriKurri, Kveta, lackadaisycal, LakeFlyPie, Lamazeroo, Lambethlil, laptopwieldingharpy, LaVitaBellissima, Leafmould, lemontop, LemonBreeland, LeonieDeSaintVire, Lilyloo, lindsell, lirogiro, Lisad123, lisalisa, LittleChiefRunnyCustard, LittleFriendSusan, Littlemefi, Livismum, llynnnn, Lucewheel, luisgarcia, madcow78, MadameDefarge, MadeleineMorrow, MaggieMcVitie,

MaggotMummy, magpieC, Mamij, MangoLangoTango, markstretch, maybeyoushoulddrive, MayCanary, Mechavivzilla, Melliebobs, Melty, Merrylegs, mignonette, MILdesperandum, mildred37, missorinoco, Mmmmmchocolate, Molecule, Mominatrix, moocowmrs, Moominmammashandbag, MorningGromit, motherofsnortpigs, mothershipg, MrsHowardRoark, MrsJohnDeere, MrsKwazii, mrspink27, Mrspnut, MsInterpret, muddledsheep, mum2twoloudbabies, MumMoselle, Mummybookworm, mumnosGOLDisbest, nancerama, Naoko, Needsomesunshine, neolara, NettoSuperstar, nextphase, NiceBiscuits, nipitinthebud, NoKnownAllergies, Nomoreminibreaks, NorksAreMessy, northender, Nowwearefour, ouryve, ovenglove, OvO, Parisbanana, Pasanna, Peachsmuggler, PetiteRaleuse, PhylisStein, Pinkforever, PinkPepper, Pinner35, Pootles2010, PoppadomPreach, Poppedcorn, Poppyamex, pounamu, pregnabrain, pregnantpause, ProfYaffle, PseudoBadger, PuddleLuscious, Purplegeekygirl, Questioneverythingtwice, Quotationist, r2peepoo, RaspberryLemonPavlova, readysteadymummy, reastie, rhetorician, rockinhippy, Rooble, RoobyMurray, Roseformeplease, Rotter, RunnersTipple, Ruprekt, SachaF, sarahbanshee, ScienceRocks, Scootergrrrl, SecretNutellaFix, SharpObject, ShipsCat, shrinkingnora, sideburnsalawiggins, Sittingbull, sjs152, SlimJimBra, Slubberdegullion, snowballinashoebox, Snoworneahva, soapnuts, someone, Somersaults, sparkleandshine78, Sparkles23, Spirael, SquirtedPerfumeUpNoseInBoots, Starfishkiss,

starlight36, StarryEyedMama, StellaMarie,
stopeatingthatmud, strandednomore,
studyingstudying, SugarandSpite, SuiGeneris,
summerintherosegarden, sunshineonarainyday,
Susandp123, Susieloopy, tasmaniandevilchaser,
Terrywoganstrousers, TheFowlandthePussycat,
TheHeirofSlytherin, TheKnackeredChef,
TheLaineyWayIsEssex, TheRealFellatio,
Theressomethingaboutmarie, thewhistler,
theycallmestacey, Thursdaynextismyhero,
Timewastingonhere, TimrousBeastie,
Titsalinabumsquash, Tommychoochoo,
Tootssweet, Treats, Tri10, tunnocksteacake,
Twittertotter, twolittlebundles, Twonker,
Umami, UnChartered, Vajazzler, Viewofthehills,
wannabedomesticgoddess, Weblette,
Welovecouscous, wentshopping, WheresMyCow,
whojamaflip, WhoYaGonnaCallFillybuster,
whyriskit, Wigeon, wolvesdidit, Woodlands,
woody17, worldgonecrazy, YouSexyBeauty,
yoyo123, Zanz1bar, zipzap, zonedout,
ZuleikaJambiere, Zwitterion

**Mums who offered their kitchens
and their time**
Ruth Ashby, Emma Barrington, Liz Bird, Michèle
Dée, Innes Ebert, Malini Mehra, Anita Mullane

Other helpers
Alex and Sophia; Destiny; Eleanor and Beatrice;
Elizabeth and Sophia; Faber and Soren; Gabrielle;
Io and Abe; Kieran; Lillie; Lucas, Fiona and
Kristen; Mia; Ned

Resources

Meal planning

eattheseasons.co.uk
Tells you what's in the shops, so you can work out tasty and cheap meal plans.
england.lovefoodhatewaste.com
Useful ideas for reducing waste as well as your weekly spend on food.
food52.com
Great words of wisdom, recipes, and ideas for cooking and feeding kids.
justbento.com
Offers exquisite packed lunch ideas.
riverford.co.uk
Weekly inspiration on what to make with your fruit and veg.

Healthy eating

bda.uk.com
Includes a series of practical 'food fact' information sheets written by dietitians.
childrensfoodtrust.org.uk
Advice, training and support for feeding children.
infantandtoddlerforum.org
Useful advice on feeding babies and toddlers, and information on common nutritional problems.
nhs.uk/change4life
Practical advice on food and maintaining a healthy lifestyle for parents and children.
vegsoc.org
Information and support for vegetarians.
webmd.com/fda
Handy hints for freezing and refrigerating food.

Useful tools

convert-me.com
Offers a handy online calculator that converts measurements from kilograms to pounds and ounces, and so on.
eatyourbooks.com
Lets you search online for recipes from the cookbooks on your shelves.

Retailers

cakecraftshop.co.uk
For all things related to cake baking.
ikea.co.uk
For a once-yearly shop for bumper supplies of napkins, crispbreads and croustades.
janeasher.com
More cake stuff...
lakeland.co.uk
This website is addictive... For things you never knew you needed!
natoora.co.uk
A wonderful online retailer which supplies many of Britain's top restaurants.
tkmaxx.com
Good-value homeware, for when you need to invest in a new casserole dish.
suma.coop
Lets you buy quality food in bulk (with neighbours and friends) for less.

Index

A Note on the Authors

mumsnet was the brainchild of Justine Roberts, who came up with the idea of a website to help parents pool information and advice after a disastrous first family holiday with her one-year-old twins. She persuaded friends Carrie Longton and Steven Cassidy to help her build the Mumsnet site, which is now regarded as one of the most influential online women's communities in Britain.

Claire and Lucy McDonald are both bloggers, mothers and journalists. Claire worked as an editor and writer at *The Times* for more than ten years, and Lucy has made regular appearances on television. They have an award-winning family food blog, Crumbs Food, and an immensely popular YouTube channel. This is their first recipe book, in conjunction with Mumsnet. They are each married with two children and they live in different corners of London.